How
to Write
a Better
Thesis
or Report

How to Write a Better Thesis or Report

David Evans

MELBOURNE
UNIVERSITY
PRESS

First published 1995
Reprinted 1996

Designed and typeset by Jan Schmoeger/Designpoint
in 10.5/14 point ITC New Baskerville
Printed in Malaysia by
SRM Production Services Sdn. Bhd. for
Melbourne University Press, Carlton, Victoria 3053

National Library of Australia Cataloguing-in-Publication entry

Evans, D. G. (David G.).
How to write a better thesis or report.

Bibliography.
Includes index.
ISBN 0 522 84665 3.

1. Report writing. 2. Dissertations, Academic. I. Title.

808.066

Foreword

The thesis remains, for obvious reasons, the single most important piece of writing a graduate student produces. It is very often the hardest part of the process of obtaining a higher degree—the research itself being more a pleasure than an exacting task.

The advent of word processors and graphics packages has enabled students to produce high quality theses. Thankfully we are nearing the end of the period where photographs are glued to A4 sheets, where addenda and corrections are pasted inside the front cover. We are entering a new period where the library copy will be a CD (or whatever more stable technology supersedes it) and where examiners will receive the thesis by e-mail.

However, all these facilities for high quality thesis production have not changed the basic task of the graduate student. Organizing one's research results into a coherent framework in concise clear English is the final test of the apprentice scholar's readiness to be promoted to the ranks of master.

David Evans is one such master with an impressive record of postgraduate supervision. He is well placed to address the difficulties of writing a thesis, especially for the science or engineering student in whom the written word often produces a form of paralysis not described in the medical textbooks. Such students may not have written an essay since high school and any papers from their research that have already appeared will be heavily influenced by the style of the supervisor. Increasingly, universities are realizing that some disciplines have evolved in a way to minimize the teaching of written and oral communication skills and that these skills must be taught in addition to the traditional professional ones. If universities tackle this task, it may be that David's book will be redundant in ten years time; as a supervisor (if not as an author) I am sure he would approve.

In the meantime, it is abundantly obvious that the ideas and suggestions contained in the following pages will be of enormous value to present-day graduate students and to supervisors who might like to consider making it compulsory reading for their own students.

Professor L. R. White
Dean
School of Graduate Studies
The University of Melbourne

Contents

Preface

When I wrote my masters thesis in the early 1950s, I had no guidebook to tell me how to put it together, and no critical supervisor to tell me what would and would not do. When I started supervising other people's theses some years later, there was still no guidebook, either for supervisor or student. I learnt supervising on the job. Since then, I have written many reports and papers, and have successfully supervised the writing of thirty-four masters-by-research and PhD theses, and numerous honours and masters-by-coursework research reports. The first half of my supervising career was in fuel technology and chemical engineering, and the second in environmental planning. As a result I have supervised research projects spanning a great range of topics. Despite this great variety, I found that environmental students experienced the same problems in putting together their theses as engineering students, and that my advice took a similar turn.

Much of this advice was on the minutiae of presentation, and on what constituted a critical approach. However, it became clearer and clearer to me that the theses that caused examiners no trouble were the ones in which the structure was clear and logical. During my ten years as a member of the international editorial board of the journal *Fuel* I discovered that seasoned research workers were often little better at writing to a structure than students were, and my advice to them was nearly always of a structural kind. Gradually the rules for writing reports and theses with a sound structure crystallized in my mind. Finally, it dawned on me that I, too, would write better and more quickly if I followed my own rules! The challenge to produce the guidebook that *I* never had grew in my mind.

As the idea developed, I examined the reference sheets handed out at the libraries of both The University of Melbourne and Monash University to students who enquired about books to assist in writing assignments and theses. I also examined the books on this topic for sale at Melbourne University Bookroom. The books fell into two classes. Most of them were about *good writing*, usually directed to the humanities student. Style and presentation were foremost, and structure was dealt with very lightly or not at all. A few were about carrying out the whole research project, with material relating to writing occupying only a small part. Structure, which is the preoccupation of this book, was generally dealt with in only a page or two. I was encouraged by my survey to proceed with my writing. This book is the result. Although it had its genesis in the writing of theses, its ideas are just as applicable to the whole range of papers, assignments and reports dealing with research in the physical, biological and social sciences.

I have illustrated many points by referring to incidents that actually occurred during the writing of theses. To preserve anonymity, I have generally not used the real names of students. However, where it was necessary to describe the subject matter of the thesis in some detail I have given the full names of the students and references to their theses.

I dedicate this book to the students who have written theses for masters or doctoral research projects under my sole or joint supervision: David Allardice, John Ball, Roger Boulton, Steven Bradford, Catherin Bull, Jack Chiodo, Winson Chow, Maxine Cooper, Jerry de Gryse, Peter Drohan, Leigh Glover, John Harris, Ralph Higgins, Vineeta Hoon, George Hooper, Peter

Kas, Robert King, Liu Guo Ying, Ian Muirhead, Amru Nazif, Ian Nuberg, Awad Oussa, Eric Palmer, Geoff Rees, John Rowney, Peter Russ, Jan Schapper, Tony Stevenson, Geoff Thomas, Colina Thomson, Van Vo Nguyen and Mark Whitmore. They patiently tried out my suggestions, and together we found out what worked and what didn't.

I thank my colleague Laurie Cosgrove for her contribution to the book. She not only read the first draft and made valuable comments on it, but also contributed to some of the ideas. I also thank Jean Dunn of Melbourne University Press, who suggested many improvements to the text, and cured me of a few bad literary habits.

December 1994   David Evans

If it's not written, it's not research.

1 Introduction

One of the examiners of Joe's thesis rang me to say that it 'read like a novel'. Looking back, I don't think this was a particularly apt simile, as a novel has a different purpose and requires different skills, but I certainly knew what he meant. The story developed surely and clearly; Joe always knew where he was going; and at the end it was completely clear what he had achieved, what his conclusions were, and how they responded to the aim he had announced at the beginning of the thesis. Needless to say he passed, without any fuss.

The skills required to report the results of research or investigations are more straightforward than those of the novelist. At least they *should* be, because the writers have a very straightforward task: to convey to the reader in a convincing way what they have found out. In practice it is rather more difficult. I can recollect only one or two students who had the gift of getting it all down with ease, and with little criticism from me, their supervisor. Most of them needed this criticism and got it, and produced theses that the examiners passed. My aim in this book is to write down in a reasonably systematic way what I have been telling them.

Chapters 2 to 5 show you how to get started, and what decisions to make before you start. Chapters 6 to 12 show you how to tackle the various parts of a thesis and bring it to the point of submission. Although this book is principally about writing theses, the same ideas apply to reports and papers, which also report the results of an investigation or a piece of research. Chapter 13 deals with the modifications in approach required for reports and papers because of their differences in scope, purpose, readership and length. Chapter 14 suggests some ways of dealing with the tricky problem of joint authorship.

I am assuming from the outset that you will be writing your own thesis or report on a word processor. In making this assumption I differ from virtually all previous books on this subject. This is not a trivial difference. The word processor has opened up entirely new ways of tackling the problem of thesis and report writing, and you owe it to yourself to take advantage of them.

Finally, before you start, a word of warning. I have been handing draft chapters of this book to students for just over a year now. I find that those who are well into their writing get immediate benefit from the ideas in it. However, those who are just starting out find it harder to relate to what I am saying. Evidently the full impact comes only when you are starting to understand the problems by becoming immersed in them. If you are at an early stage, I suggest you first read Chapters 2 and 3. When you get to Chapter 4, which introduces you to the power of the word processor, you will probably find that there are more ideas than you can absorb straight away, because much of it will not take on an edge of reality until you are well into your writing. You may also find that you are not yet ready for some of the ideas in Chapter 5 on presentation. Don't be discouraged. I can assure you that everything in these two chapters is very important in the writing of a good thesis or report. If you read them through now, you will be ready to step off on the right foot, and you will come back to them later to check on points of detail.

2 Structure

My colleague Bill was worried about the draft thesis that had been submitted to him by Henry, one of his students, and asked me to look at it. It was certainly very difficult to know what was going on. Henry had written it straight from his log book, experiment after experiment, in chronological order:

> **Experiment No. 37:** as Experiment 36 failed to show the chemical reaction I expected, I next tried the effect of doubling the concentration of the active reagent . . .

And so on. Your task as writer is to make the outcome comprehensible to the readers, not to take them along all the highways and byways and down the cul-de-sacs that you traversed while establishing this outcome. It is essential that you structure your thesis or report in such a way that you take the reader from the aim to the conclusions in the clearest possible way.

I shall now lay out the essential features of this structure—a recipe, if you like, for making the cake and baking it. I shall describe these features in the context of writing a thesis; first the thesis itself, then individual chapters. (In Chapter 13 I shall look at the steps that would be treated somewhat differently for reports or for papers in learned journals.)

The thesis itself

I have had the good fortune to have spent half my supervisory career in an engineering department, and half in an environmental planning department, which has given me a rich variety of topics and styles to deal with. I can therefore say with some confidence that the standard thesis structure that I shall now describe is as appropriate for the social and biological sciences as for the physical sciences. While the nature of research in the humanities is different from that in the sciences,* and different forms of reportage may be appropriate, I believe that much of what I say about structure is applicable there also.†

Reports, theses and papers are similar, in that they are all reporting the results of some investigation or research and the conclusions to be drawn from them. At one extreme we might have a 2-page report on a routine investigation, say of a sample of material sent for analysis, while at the other extreme we might have a 200-page PhD thesis, reporting results of research

---

* C. Belsey, *Critical Practice*, Methuen, London, 1980.

† For example, in their book *Thesis and Assignment Writing* (John Wiley & Sons, Brisbane, 1994, 2nd edn) J. Anderson and M. Poole give checklists for the two types of thesis (pp. 143–5) which I paraphrase below. Despite the different procedures used, the structures of the the two types of thesis are quite similar.

Thesis on Empirical/Experimental Study	Thesis on Analytical/Literary Study
Problem	**Objective**
The problem	Purpose of the study
Significance of the problem	Contribution of study to knowledge
Relationship to previous work	Evaluation of previous studies
Derivation of hypotheses	
Procedures	**Procedures**
Design of own experiments or work	Assumptions
Results of own work	Sources
	Documentation
Analysis	**Analysis**
Analysis of results	Analysis of facts
	Evaluation of material
Conclusions	**Conclusions**

that changed direction several times in the first couple of years as the researcher came to understand the area better. However, despite differences in length, readership, purpose and so on, the writing will always conform to the same structure: at the start there will be a statement of the problem under investigation, in the middle will be an account of the investigation into this problem, and at the end conclusions will be drawn.

The sequencing of items should follow the logic flow of this pathway, as shown in Figure 1. It should consist of four parts, some of which might contain more than one chapter.

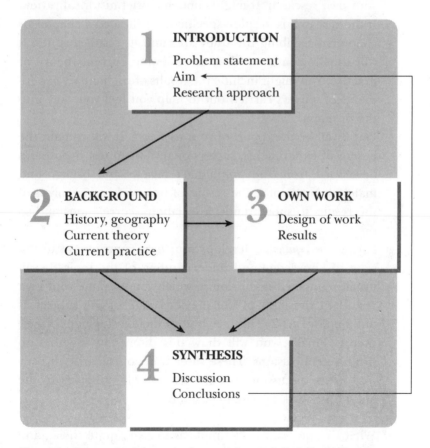

Figure 1 Structure of theses in the experimental disciplines (Reports may be structured slightly differently, see Chapter 13)

- Part 1 is the *introduction*. Don't mess around in it. Quite literally, it should introduce the research. You should start by outlining the problem you intend to investigate, then state the aim of the research to be reported, and then outline the approach you will use to achieve this aim. Two or three pages is enough for this—I was once asked to examine a masters thesis in which the aim didn't appear until page 40, part way through Chapter 3. Plenty of scope for the reader to get lost there!
- Part 2 is the *background* required before you can describe your own research. It might contain a brief historical review. If the research is location-specific you will need a chapter or chapters describing the study area and its characteristics. It will usually contain a chapter reviewing current theory or practice. You might include the results of preliminary experiments or surveys carried out to help you feel your way into the problem.
- Part 3 will be the report of your *own work*. It will contain the design of experiments, surveys or reviews to test hypotheses developed from the preliminary reviews and background material. Next come the results of this work, and analysis of the results to show trends, associations, correlations and so on.
- Part 4, the *synthesis*, develops your own contribution to the state of knowledge and understanding of the topic. It will usually contain a discussion in which you examine your own results in the light of the previous state of the subject as outlined in Part 2. This may lead to the development of new theory. Finally, you will draw this discussion together to produce conclusions. These should, of course, arise directly out of the discussion, but they should also respond to the aim of the work as stated in Part 1.

What I've just said is so simple as to seem quite trivial, and you may say, 'Well of course that is what I would do in any case'. It doesn't work like that! Almost invariably confusion and wasted effort (not to mention unfavourable referees' or examiners' reports) are associated with major deviations from the above scheme. Conversely, I can say that if you stick to it you will write a clear and comprehensible thesis or report. I will deal with these four parts in Chapters 6 to 11. My aim in this chapter is to convince you that you should neglect none of them, and that you should develop them in the order I have just given.

One last thing: how many chapters should there be? If there are four main parts, each containing one to three chapters, we should not expect more than eight or ten chapters. If you have more, you should suspect that some are really only sections of chapters, and you should attempt some consolidation. My university once asked me to report on a request for financial assistance to publish a thesis as a book. It had around thirty chapters! The simple and coherent structure shown in Figure 1 was totally obscured by the proliferation of chapters with seemingly arbitrary titles. The effect of this was total disintegration, and I was surprised that the examiners had passed it.

The individual chapters

Gail kept handing me chapters in which she said everything three times. She started off with a summary of what she was going to do; then she wrote the body of the chapter, describing what she was doing; and finally she ended with a summary of what she had done. This was not only unbelievably *boring* but also unhelpful, because it was never clear *why* she was doing what she did in any particular chapter or, at the end, where it had got us. Her 'introductions' were just tables of contents, and her 'conclusions' were just summaries.

Just as the thesis itself must be properly structured to ensure that the reader always knows exactly what is going on, so must individual chapters. Why is this particular chapter there? What is its function in the thesis? You must make this absolutely clear. The best way to ensure this is to write a formal introduction to every chapter. Follow this with the business of the chapter itself, then a formal conclusion. I know that many advisers consider this to be a rather stilted, over-formal approach, and skilful writers can certainly get away with no formal introductions and conclusions. This doesn't mean that they can do away with introductions and conclusions to chapters; rather that they do it less formally and obviously. Most of us don't have such writing skills, however, and I recommend that formal introductions and conclusions be included.

What do I mean by a formal introduction? A simple rule worth following is that it should contain three paragraphs. In the first paragraph you create a link back to the earlier parts of the thesis, especially the previous chapter, to make it obvious why we need the chapter. In the second paragraph you crystallize this by stating the aim of the chapter, what *function* it is to perform in the thesis. Then in the third paragraph you outline how you intend to achieve this aim. This third paragraph often has the 'table of contents' format that so many writers think constitutes an introduction. But it is only one part of the introduction, and without the other two parts the reader struggles for a sense of direction. (Incidentally, writers sometimes literally give it as a table of contents. This is far from helpful. The reader needs to know not only what you will be dealing with in the chapter, but also the logical connection between the various sections.)

After the introduction comes the main body of the chapter. Its precise contents and structure will depend on the type of chapter you are writing and the type of research you are reporting. Nevertheless, it is important that it flow logically from the purpose of the chapter, as stated in its introduction, to its conclusions. This typically involves three or four major sections. If you have more than six sections in a chapter, including the introduction and conclusion, you may be fairly sure that you haven't got the structure right.

Every chapter in a report or thesis should have a conclusion. The reader needs to share with the writer a sense of what has been achieved, what is established now that wasn't established at the beginning of the chapter. And the conclusion should, of course, respond to the stated aim or purpose of the chapter. There may be some exceptions, for example descriptive chapters outlining information on the characteristics of a study area. But chapters that should definitely have strong conclusions are reviews of theory, reviews of available research methods, reports of results, and discussion (the conclusions here may constitute the conclusions to the whole thesis or report).

To my continuing surprise, I have found that students often have difficulty with conclusions. They tend to write summaries of what was in the chapter; when I say to them, 'But what did you conclude from this chapter?' they reply, 'That's what I've given you'. Then I write down *my* version of their conclusions to illustrate what I mean. Usually, they can immediately see the difference, and go on to write a much superior version themselves. A summary states *what* you found out, whereas a conclusion states the *significance* of what you found out (but don't get ahead of yourself; it must be in the context of that part of the thesis that the reader has already read). A conclusion has to respond to the statement of purpose of the chapter, whereas a summary is just a potted version of what is in the chapter.

A test for structural integrity

How do you know whether your thesis or report will hang together? Obviously it will help to do an outline of the whole work before you start, consisting of a list of chapter headings and the subsidiary section headings, as might appear in a table of contents. Many word-processing packages have routines for doing this, which can be used to advantage. However, this is a fairly blunt instrument, as headings don't tell you much.

I have found that a far more powerful test for structural integrity is to attempt to write the introductions to each chapter (better still the introductions *and* conclusions), using the scheme given earlier in this chapter. String these introductions together, and it will be obvious whether there are logic gaps, repetitions, back-trackings etc. in your basic outline. Then fix these up and restructure the outline before you attempt to write the text itself.

The act of writing will almost inevitably change your structural scheme—you will find that things that you thought would emerge fail to do so, or that other things emerge unexpectedly. When your hands run away on the keyboard as your creative subconscious takes over and makes a mockery of your careful structural planning, you should ask yourself whether the new version is heading in a better direction. How can you tell? Try the string-of-introductions trick again, but this time use introductions that accommodate your new direction. If it works better, scrap the old structure and replace it with the new. If it doesn't, scrap the new material and try again. It may be that this new material is worth keeping (never ignore the workings of the subconscious mind when doing research), but the test reveals that it is in the wrong place. If you think this could be so, cut it out and paste it temporarily where you think it may belong, promising yourself that you will work on it when you get to that new chapter.

3 Getting Started

Len was having trouble starting his thesis. He had been reading the literature on his topic for quite a while, and decided that the first thing he had to write was a review of this literature (more of this in Chapter 7). I told him that I would like to see an outline of how he expected to tackle it in one week's time. Two weeks later nothing had appeared. I went to see him, and asked what the problem was. 'No problem', he replied, 'It's just that I still have seven more papers to read. When I've read them I'll start writing'. I reminded him that he'd told me two weeks ago that he had only two more papers to read, and then he would start writing. He explained that, while reading one of these two, he'd turned up several more papers. He then showed me a little metal card box containing a card for every paper he'd read, with its details and his abstract of what it was saying. I asked him how many cards were in it. 'A hundred and twenty, with seven more to come.' He was never going to start. He told himself that finding new papers was the reason, but it was clear that the problem lay deeper.

This won't be a long chapter but, if you are one of those who can't seem to start writing, it might be the most important one in the book—one postgraduate student I knew had done excellent work for her masters degree but never got the degree because she could not get her thesis started. Why does this problem occur, and how can it be tackled?

Analysis of the problem

Research is not a completely rational process. In nearly every research project I have been connected with, the conclusions contained some quite unexpected elements. In most projects the *aim* of the work changed during the course of it, sometimes several times. Often I've had students come to me and say that their 'experiments had failed', but when we had absorbed the implications of the supposed failure new hypotheses emerged that resulted in breakthroughs in their research. On several occasions quite remarkable conclusions were staring the student (and me) in the face, yet we failed to see them for weeks or even months because we were so hooked on what we *expected* to find out.

In the classical application of the 'scientific method' the researcher is supposed to develop a hypothesis, then design a crucial experiment to test it. If the hypothesis withstands this test a generalization is then argued for, and an advance in understanding has been made. But where did the hypothesis come from in the first place? I have a colleague whose favourite question is 'Why is this so?', and I've seen this innocent question spawn brilliant research projects on quite a few occasions. Thus, research is a peculiar mixture of creative thinking (hypothesis generation, musing over the odd and surprising), and rational thinking (design and execution of crucial experiments, analysis of results in terms of existing theory).

I have been advocating up to this point that in structuring the reports of research we should put aside the creative approach to writing and use only a rational approach. Yet all of us know that we do write creatively, at least in the fine detail of it. We talk of our pens (or fingers on the keyboard) running ahead of our brains, as if our brains were the rational bit of us and our fingers the creative bit. This is, of course, nonsense, and we know it, yet the experience is there.

Wrestling with this problem has led me to the view that all writing, like all research, involves the tension between the creative and the rational parts of our brains. It is this tension that makes it so hard for us to start writing, that sometimes gives us 'writer's block', and that probably leads some of us to take refuge in 'thesisese' (see Chapter 5). To get started, we must resolve the tension. I shall describe two ways for doing this, one to use as soon as you start your research project, and the other to use if you don't start writing until you have almost completed it.

Integrating the writing with the research

I nearly gave this book the title *You Could Write Up Now*, because that is what supervisors used to say to research students who had virtually finished their research and were ready to begin the writing phase. The reason for this break between the two phases of the work was clear enough. Typing from a manuscript on a typewriter to produce a finished thesis was a job for experts. If one made a mistake, it meant retyping a whole page. Flaws in the logic of the argument could not be remedied without retyping a whole chapter. The student had to get the manuscript right, once and for all, and *hand it over to the typist*. 'Writing-up' was, therefore, a discrete task, not really feasible until the research had finished.

This is no longer the case. An alternative model for writing has been made possible by the word processor, and the research and the writing can now go on simultaneously. It will be clear from nearly everything that I have to say in this book that I believe this new model of the research/writing process to be preferable.

But how can you describe work that has not yet been done? And why might the attempt be beneficial? These seem to be fair questions. However, they presuppose a rational model of research. As I have just argued, this model does not correspond with our experience. The assumption behind the questions is that the researcher's own work (experiments, surveys, interviews etc.) constitutes the real research, that the reading and mastering of the literature is not part of the research, that listening to others is not part of the research, and that being provoked into thinking outside the 'usual' framework of the topic is not research. If you are a postgraduate student getting your first experiences of research, you might think that these things are, at best, only marginal to your research. So, let me ask another question: Is the formulation of your hypotheses part of your research? If it were not, you could not design your research program (see Chapter 8). *But it is these other processes that enable you to form your hypotheses.* If you accept that I am right, would it not be beneficial to try to document, in a rational way, the non-rational, creative processes that led you to your hypotheses? You will have to do this in the end, anyway, so why not try it right now, before you have done any surveys or interviews, or carried out any experiments?

There are three potential benefits. I have mentioned the first of them above: if you have to argue out your hypotheses in writing, it will help you to think more constructively about them. It will help you to identify the processes that enabled you to formulate these hypotheses, and you will know that you will have to bring these out in your reviews of existing theory or practice (see Chapter 7). All of this should lead to better hypotheses, and better design of your research program. The second benefit is the one I have been stressing in this chapter: if you start to write at an early stage you will be well into your writing before you have done your own surveys or experiments. Therefore, you will not be faced with the formidable task of 'getting started' on your writing when you have all but finished your research, because you will have started long ago. The third benefit is that it will help you to give shape to your project, including the report on it, at an early stage. To explain this, I shall now outline how you might go about it.*

---

* This method, and the example I will use shortly, owe a lot to my colleague Laurie Cosgrove, who has pushed the idea further than I have myself. We have jointly supervised some projects using it. It works.

I described in Chapter 2 how you should structure a thesis or report. When you read that chapter you probably assumed that this was something you would do after you had finished your research. However, if you re-read Chapter 2, you will see that you could devise the structure I recommended there at a very early stage of the work. To do this, first write a draft of your introductory chapter—the problem statement, the aim, and the steps in the approach you think you might take to achieve the aim. These steps then define succeeding chapters. (You may not feel too confident about writing this introduction, because you suspect that it will have to be modified later, as you get into your work. In this you are almost certainly correct, but that should not prevent you from writing a draft introduction. What you are trying to do is 'get started'.)

With a bit of imagination you can now have a go at writing the aims of most of the chapters, and even some of the method steps you might use to achieve these aims. As an example, suppose you decide to do some research on ecotourism. Your supervisor, no doubt, will ask what the aim of your research is. Probably you will have trouble with this question, as you became interested in ecotourism only because you suspected that there were some inherent problems in the idea. However, as a way of proceeding, you settle on the following tentative aim for your project: 'To establish whether ecotourism will help to preserve ecological systems'. Starting to write will help you to clarify this aim. You can see straight away how difficult it will be to write a critical review of the literature on ecotourism at this stage. But what you can do quite easily is review the appropriate background. There are some things that you will need to be familiar with to achieve your aim: (1) Definitions of ecotourism; (2) History of ecotourism: Where did the idea come from? What has happened since? (3) What are the problems with ecotourism? (this would be an expansion of your problem statement); (4) What has been the response to date from tour operators and from governments? When you have read the literature and written a piece on each of these you will be far better informed about your project, and may have revised your aim. You will certainly be in a much better position to devise surveys of potential ecotourists, and interviews with tour operators. The writing will not be wasted. You will incorporate much of it in your final thesis, although you will no doubt make many changes before that.

Thinking your way into your project like this will help you to write a tentative structure for the first part of your thesis. Of course, you will have a big blank in the last two chapters, which will just read 'Discussion' and 'Conclusions'. But you now have enough to draw up as a tentative table of contents.

Next, get a loose-leaf folder, with a set of card dividers. Paste the structures for each chapter on individual card dividers. Insert the draft table of contents for the whole report in the front. Then decide which chapter or section of a chapter you could tackle first, and start writing. (As you can see from the ecotourism example, it is better at this stage to write a 'factual' chapter first, rather than one where you will be forced to make many interpretations or judgements.) As you write you should try to follow the 'rational' structure you have predetermined. But once you start writing to this 'rational' outline you should let your fingers do the talking: slip uninhibitedly into creative-writing mode. When you have written the chapter, insert it behind the appropriate card divider as the first version of that chapter. If it is not a complete chapter, write a few notes on the missing sections to indicate how you envisage that you will construct the whole chapter, and how the material you have written fits in. Every time you go to a meeting with your supervisor or supervisors, take the folder with you. *It is the latest draft of your report or thesis.*

As a result of your own work and thinking, and your discussions on the progress of the project with your supervisors and others, you will no doubt see many gaps and inconsistencies in your draft structure. Revise the structure to deal with these problems whenever necessary, drawing up a new table of contents and new chapter structures and introductions, and sort your folder into the new structure. You will retain some of the material you wrote previously, although you might put it in different chapters. For the time being, put any material for which you cannot find a home in an appendix at the back, labelled with a title (you will probably reject it eventually, but it might be useful later). As results start to emerge from your own work, they will take their place quite easily as one or more 'Results' chapters. Then you will have many ideas and even arguments about what they signify, and drafts of the 'Discussion' and 'Conclusions' chapters will start to emerge (I shall discuss a process for getting these into shape in Chapters 10 and 11). These drafts will also be tucked behind the appropriate card dividers. One day you will walk into a meeting with your supervisors, and you will all realize that the report has taken its final shape—all it needs is the final working through to turn it into the first draft of the complete work. I hope I have made it sound easy. If you do it this way, it is.

Writing after you have done your own work

I mentioned earlier Len's problem in starting to write his thesis. When he wrote his thesis over twenty years ago, word processors had not been invented, and the integrated research/writing process that I have just discussed was hardly possible. Instead, we had the 'research first and write later' model of thesis writing.

Despite the flexibility now offered by the word processor, it seems that old habits die hard amongst professional research workers and supervisors: many researchers still leave their writing until after they have finished their research. Of course, it is research students who most often find themselves in trouble when they do this, because this is their first piece of sustained research. However, experienced research workers often have the same problem. One professional research worker I know, when faced with a writing deadline such as the appointed submission date for a report or for a conference paper, does exactly what Len did. Instead of getting on with it, he invents all sorts of extra reviews or reading or analysis that has to be done, and rings up the intended recipient for an extension of time. Then, when it is clear that no more extensions are available and it is almost too late to meet the final deadline, he sits down in a state of heightened awareness and writes all night to produce the report. Many of us use milder versions of this ploy on occasions, myself included. It is a way of making our creative minds work overtime. But it is dangerous: one day it might let us down, and in any case it always leaves us with no time to reflect on, then revise, what we have written. Above all, the structure of the argument is likely to suffer.

I did manage to get Len going eventually. This is how I did it: I asked him how many important ideas he had identified in those 120 papers, ideas that had taken the theory of his topic along another step. To my surprise, he replied almost immediately that there were only four, and explained them. I saw that somehow his subconscious mind had been working on those 120 papers, sorting them, organizing them, ordering them. I told him that these four ideas would doubtless provide the titles of four sections of his review of existing theory, and suggested he start writing on this basis. He came back in two weeks with a brilliant review of the theory that scarcely needed any change.

My advice to Len enabled him to get started because it gave him a structure to write to. I think we were a bit lucky, as the review of existing theory is not an easy chapter to start on. Nevertheless, it did work, because it enabled him to resolve the tension between his rational, conscious thinking and his creative, unconscious thinking.

To *harness* this tension you must first devise a logical structure for the whole thesis or report, using the general format outlined in Chapter 2. As I noted there, a good way to ensure that the structure is sound is to write the introductions to each chapter, then string them together to see whether the report develops logically. The tentative table of contents (chapter headings and section headings within chapters) should reflect this logic. Then, start to write. I suggest that you start with the introductory chapter that describes why you are doing the research, what your aim is, and how you intend to achieve it. If you are having trouble with this chapter, you most likely have not yet got the aim of the whole project right. Put it aside for the moment, and start with another. A good idea is to start with a factual chapter, one describing the study area, or the rationale for selecting a research method, or the design of experiments or questionnaires. These are chapters in which the rational side of writing will predominate, and the creative side will not provide a stumbling block.*

Again, follow the structure that you have devised with the rational side of your brain but, once you start the writing itself, allow the creative side of your brain to work through the argument for you. When you have finished writing for the day, save what you have written. Then go to bed, and sleep on it (the very existence of this expression is evidence that our subconscious thinking processes keep working even when all rational thinking has been switched off). Your first task the next day is to look at the chapter outline, then read, on the screen, the chapter as it stands. As well as picking up typographical and grammatical errors you will readily see the results of the tension between creative writing and rational structure. If you find that they are at odds, one of them must give. Either your original rational structure was wrong, in which case you must alter it, or your creative thinking has taken you on a wild-goose chase, in which case you must cut the errant material out. But you now

---

* It is not a good idea to start with a 'critical review' of existing theory, as used to be fashionable, indeed compulsory. How one could be 'critical' in these circumstances is quite beyond me. This is probably the hardest chapter for an inexperienced student to write, as it demands a strong resolution of the tension between the creative and rational sides of writing. (In fact, as I discuss in Chapter 7, I don't believe one should have a chapter headed 'Literature Review' in a thesis, anyway.)

have inputs from both sides of your brain, and can sit in judgement on the outcome.

Very soon you will find that you have written a chapter, or at least some sections of one. You have started! You, like Len, will have no problem in continuing with the process of writing, gradually building up a complete thesis or report.

4 Making Your Word Processor Work for You

When researchers first began to use word processors, they used them rather like typewriters: they still wrote a manuscript by hand, and handed it to the typist for typing. But now they had the luxury of treating the typescript as a draft that could easily be changed— by marking it up and handing it back to the typist for revision.

All this has changed. Most of my fellow academics do all their own word processing. All of my research students have done so for some years now. Most undergraduate assignments are produced by the students on word processors. Many professional consultants and officers in government departments produce all but the final versions of their reports on word processors at their own desks. This has profoundly affected the way research can be carried out and reported.

I am assuming in this chapter that you have basic knowledge of how to operate word-processing programs. To produce a good thesis or report, you will need far more than this, but the word-processing programs commonly available today include all the required features. I will now suggest how to get the best out of your word processor; to make it work for you.

Presentation

Reflect on the aims of the writers of word-processing programs. They didn't just sit down at their desks and say, 'Wouldn't it be nice to write this feature or that capability into our program'. Instead, they had many sessions with experienced writers, typists, typesetters, book editors and so on, and listed all the features that might be desirable. They than estimated the computer memory that might be required, and put the features in some order of priority. This led them to reject some features that were desirable but not feasible within the constraints of available computer power, and they finally produced a program that embodied the best combination of desirable features at that time. Experience by users revealed the limitations of the programs and, as computer power increased, the programmers produced new versions that overcame the problems, and built in new features. We have now reached the stage where programs are so sophisticated that it is almost beyond the power of single individuals to make use of all the features. I have laboured this point to indicate that you should approach the learning of the capabilities of programs by saying, 'This is what I want to do; I know the programmers will have provided me with the capability. All I have to do is find it'.

Nowhere is this more apparent than in the question of presentation. The program can't do your creative thinking for you (not yet, anyway!), but it is very good at helping you to get things down in a good and clear format. More recent programs check your spelling for you, and even make suggestions about your grammar. Programs can also do footnotes for you, and help you with your list of references and your table of contents.

Formatting and style sheets

At secretarial colleges, typists are taught the importance of using a clear and systematic *format.** You* will have to learn to do this

---

* 'Format' here means the physical layout of the thesis or report. It includes such things as: the choice of type for both normal text and headings; spacing before and after headings and between paragraphs and lines; page margins; justification of lines; headers or footers, including page numbering; choice of reference system; layout of tables and figures, including their captions, and so on.

for yourself. For example, you should put all chapter headings on a new page, using the same style and format. You should give all major section headings within a chapter the same style and format: one that is less obtrusive than that of the chapter headings. You should leave the same space before all section headings. Captions to figures should all have the same style and format. All new paragraphs should have the same space before them, and should begin with the same indent (except for the first paragraph after a heading, which may have no indent at all), and so on. All this will help your readers to navigate their way through your report or thesis.

Before you start typing anything for your report or thesis, you should think about this, and devise styles and formatting rules that are appropriate for your type of report. Above all, make up your mind that, right from the outset, you will not use just any old style, with a view to tightening things up later when you are more confident about what you are doing. Begin as you mean to continue.

Fortunately, most current word-processing programs have a feature built into them that will help you to do this, while keeping the flexibility to change your styles later if you wish. It is called a *style sheet*.* This is the way it works. First, you decide on the various styles you intend to use in your document. You will have different ones for chapter headings, section headings, sub-section headings, normal text, quotations, captions to figures, indented material labelled with a bullet (large dot) or a number, and so on. You can use the styles already built into the program (default styles), or invent your own. (As I shall explain later, you should use the default *names* for the styles, even if you change the details of them.) For each *style* you will specify the typeface you wish to use (Times, Geneva etc.), type size, type character (bold, italic, outline etc.), any justification (left, right, centre) or indenting, any space before or after the paragraph,

---

* I am using the word-processing program Word 5, and will use the descriptive language of that program. Other programs may have slightly different features, or use different language to describe the same features.

and any special instructions (for example that a heading is not to appear by itself at the bottom of a page without its succeeding paragraph, or that a paragraph is not to be split between two pages). Each style is specified as a variant of a previously specified style. Usually you would start by defining the *normal* style (to be used on ordinary text), then specify other styles as variants of it. This is an important point, as I shall explain shortly. These styles are automatically collected by the program as a *style sheet* for the document you are working on.

Once you have decided on the desired styles and have specified them and entered them on your style sheet, you can start typing. As you type, you label each paragraph with the desired style. (Even a heading is a paragraph—a paragraph is merely defined by material that begins after you insert a <paragraph> or <return> marker, and ends when you insert the next <paragraph> or <return> marker.) You can make the program do this for you more or less automatically, as follows: each style can be labelled with a *next style*. For example, you give *normal* style the next-style label of normal style also, so that you will remain in normal style from paragraph to paragraph. When you come to the end of a section, you have to label the next paragraph with a style *heading 2* for a section heading, or *heading 3* for a subsection heading, but you specify the *next style* for both of these as *normal,* so that the paragraph following a heading will automatically be in normal style. As you build up your document, you will have labelled every single paragraph with some style.

In this way, you have already achieved consistency in formatting. Paragraphs will always have the same indenting, and the same space between them; all section headings will be in exactly the same style, and so on. But you have another enormous advantage. Suppose you decide, when you print out a sample page or so, that the titles for figures are not really the way you want them. If you have given all figure titles the same style, say *heading 5,* all you have to do is re-specify this style into the desired format. Every paragraph you have labelled *heading 5* will automatically be changed to the new *heading 5* style.

Another great feature is that if all styles are variants of *normal,* you can change the typeface for the whole document by merely changing the typeface of the normal style. I use this capability myself all the time. I prefer to print my documents in 12 point Times, because it gives a readable and compact printed page. However, this is not easy to read on the screen. Therefore, I type on to the screen using 12 point Geneva, which *is* easy to read on the screen. Then, before printing I change the typeface in *normal* style from Geneva to Times. Since I have based all styles on normal style, the typefaces in all of the document will be changed to Times, except where I have deliberately specified contrary instructions. You will quickly see many other ways to use this flexibility. For example, your superior or supervisor may wish to have draft material submitted double-spaced, to give room on the print-out for suggestions and corrections. Before you print the final document, you can then change *normal* from double-spaced to single-spaced. A word of warning, however: such changes may result in page breaks occurring in different places, so you must check the consequences before printing.

Finally, you can easily transfer a style sheet from one document to another. If you are working on a joint document, you can arrange for all participants to use the same style sheet from the outset. If you are collecting documents from several different authors who have used different style sheets it is not too late to bring them to a uniform style, although it will be much more laborious than if you had started off on the right foot. Recently some colleagues and I edited a book with contributions from eighteen different authors. We adopted a style sheet and forced it on every contribution before we started our editing. This was quite a task, but the flexibility it then gave us was well worth while.

Spell-checks and grammar-checks

Most word-processing programs include a routine for checking spelling. It checks every word you have typed against a dictionary built into the program. If it can't find the word (either because the word is not in the program's dictionary or because you have spelt it wrongly—sometimes because you have inadvertently omitted the space between two words), it will invite you to respond. You can respond either by ignoring the warning, and telling it to get on with its searching, or by accepting the invitation to change the word to a preferred spelling. I strongly urge you to use the spell-check. Very few people are infallible spellers or proof-readers. It is as well to have oddities questioned.

However, although the spell-check is very good at picking up typographical errors, it can't make decisions for you. Typical problems are people's names or place names, and words for which there are alternative spellings. In the case of proper names, the temptation is to tell the program to ignore its questionings, and go instead to the next area of doubt. This is a mistake. I have read several reports which were superbly free from typographical errors in normal words, but were rife with errors in the spelling of proper names (often with the same proper name spelt differently at various places). You should check any proper name the first time the spell-check comes to it and, when you are satisfied that you have got it right, add it to the dictionary installed in the program. The second problem is words for which alternative spellings are permissible (*-or* or *-our*, and *-ize* or *-ise* are the most common). The most important constraint here is that you must be consistent. Before you start, determine your preferred spellings for these words, and keep to them.

Finally, don't rely on the spell-check to proof-read for you; although it will pick up misspelt words, it won't distinguish between, for example, *there* and *their*, or *affect* and *effect*. Similarly, it won't tell you if you have left a word out.

A grammar-check, which is contained in the most recent programs, may also help. Grammar-checks operate a bit like spell-checks. They look at every sentence, and make checks such as: does it contain a verb; is it too long and complicated; does the subject agree with the verb (plural subjects must not have singular verbs); is the verb in the passive voice (permissible, but should be used sparingly); are stock phrases being used (examples: 'over and above', 'in order to', 'part and parcel'), and so on. The trouble with grammar-checks is that English is such a complex language, with such tricky grammar rules, that the program often has to 'think' for an interminable time before asking its questions. Even then it sometimes asks silly questions, and you have to be a reasonably good grammarian to know when you should ignore it and when you should pay attention to it. Consequently, most of my colleagues will not use the grammar-check.

I have persisted with it because, despite these faults, it makes me ask myself questions about grammar. In particular, I have found that I over-use the passive voice (you will not see that fault in this book, thanks to the program), and that my sentences tend to be too long and complicated. If you cannot work out what it is saying to you, don't abandon it. Instead, seek help from someone who is a better grammarian than you are. Treat the check as a critical friend, not an enemy that you should run away from. I expect that the next generation of grammar-checks will be cleverer and more user-friendly than the present ones.

References

Word-processing programs usually have referencing systems (see Chapter 5) built into them. You can stop at any point and insert a *note* (probably your word-processing program, like mine, calls them *footnotes* rather than notes, because the default setting does collect them at the foot of each page). You can give each note a number or symbol yourself, or you can ask the program to automatically number them, which is preferable. The number (or symbol) will appear as a superscript in the text, and also as a duplicate on a separate part of the screen. You are invited to type in the text of your note against this duplicate number. If later you wish to add another note higher up on the same page, all you have to do is insert a new note marker in the text. The notes will automatically renumber themselves, and you simply type in the text for the new note on the separate part of the screen. Conversely, if you delete an existing reference number from the main text, the note text that went with it will also be automatically deleted, and the other notes will be renumbered automatically.

Notes are usually collected at the end of each page as *footnotes*. When the page is printed out you will see the superscript number in the main text and the footnote text at the bottom of the page, separated from the main text by a dividing line. If you have more than one reference number on the page, the footnotes will all be collected automatically on that page. However, if you wish, you may instead collect the notes at the end of a section (for example, at the end of each chapter, as *chapter notes*) or in a consolidated listing at the end of the document (*endnotes*).

Wherever you put them, the notes have to be backed up by a consolidated alphabetical listing of all the references in them. When I am using the system of referencing that I've just described (the *numbered notes* system), I copy all notes with a reference in them on to a separate document, which I call 'References'. It is then a relatively simple matter to convert all the references in this document to a listing with authors' names first and then, using the sorting sub-routine in the word-processing program, to generate a list of references in alphabetical order.

At present, a different reference system, the *name and year* or *Harvard* system, is more popular for theses and reports than the numbered notes system. Your word-processing program will also help you to use this system, in conjunction with a reference data-base built up by either yourself or your organization using a program such as *Endnote*. In this program you build up a listing of references much like the old card-index system used by a previous generation of researchers. Each entry consists of the usual listing of author, title of article and journal, or of book or chapter of book, year of publication, and publisher and place, together with an abstract and keywords. This reference data base can be used quite independently of your thesis or report as a personal literature recording and accessing device (using author's name or keywords or title of book or journal to search for material). However, it has the great advantage that you can interface it with your report or thesis to automatically draw up the list of references at the end.

Whichever system of referencing you use, the word processor offers the advantage that it will help you to maintain the match between the references cited in the text and the references appearing in your consolidated alphabetical list of references, or bibliography. It will help to prevent you from inadvertently omitting from your list references that have been referred to in the text, and will also help to prevent you from retaining references in the list that are no longer referred to in the text. It will also automatically sort them into alphabetical order.

Tables

The more sophisticated programs have routines for constructing tables. As these routines are rather complex, you might be tempted to abandon the attempt to use them, and to construct the tables using tabs (I often find students trying to construct tables without using even tabs, but by lining up columns with the space-bar). However, if you are going to construct an appreciable number of tables, it is worth spending time to master the table routines. If you have done the tables properly, you will be able to change the typeface or size without risking a disaster, as you would with tabs. (Rarely does one see a report without at least one entry having been displaced to the wrong column; this just won't happen if you use a table routine.)

Figures

You will sometimes find theses or reports in your library with all the figures collected together at the end of each chapter, each on a separate page. This was a product of the typewriter age; you won't find them like that in a book. The word processor enables you to enter them in much the same way as in a book: as close as you can get them to the place where they are first mentioned in the written text, and not on a separate page from the text. There are three ways of doing this:

- If your word-processing package has a reasonably sophisticated graphical routine built into it, you might consider using it to draw all your figures. This method has the advantage that you can edit the figures at a later date in the light of rewriting or alteration of the text. However, you will have to accept the limitations of the graphics routine, which might be quite considerable.

- Draw all your figures using a separate specialist graphics package, and import them electronically into your text. You will not be able to edit them while they are in your word-processed text—but you can delete them, go back to the original version in the graphics package, edit that, then re-import it.

- Draw all figures by hand on separate sheets of paper, using a consistent graphical style. Leave enough space in the word-processed text to physically paste the figures in after the pages have been printed. Of course, it is rarely possible to edit these and, if you wish to change them, you will have to redraw them.

The second of these methods is probably the best, but it does mean learning how to use another complex package, and you may not have the time to do this. Whichever method you use, you should go to some trouble to ensure consistency of style within the figures, especially if there is written material actually on the figures themselves, such as labels on the axes of graphs. You should produce the titles, or captions, of all your figures, together with any explanatory material and references to sources, in a consistent style, using your word-processing package. Don't attempt to do these graphically.

Table of contents

A *table of contents* is exactly what it says: a listing of what is contained in the thesis or report. It usually includes the titles of each chapter, with a *very* brief listing under each title of what is in the chapter. It functions as a map of the thesis or report— what is in it, how its various parts relate to each other, and how to find your way around it. It is placed at the front of the report, and you may expect it to be read first. The table of contents should not be confused with an *index*, which is a listing of important words and ideas appearing in the work, given in alphabetical order. Its function is to help anyone to check whether a subject they are interested in is dealt with in the work and, if it is, to find it. An index is located at the end of the work, and will not be read before the work itself; in fact, it is unlikely to be read systematically at all. The most recent word-processing programs have routines for generating both tables of contents and indexes. I shall discuss only tables of contents here, as it is most unusual to have an index in a thesis or report.

If you give your chapter titles the style *heading 1,* your section headings the style *heading 2,* your sub-section headings the style *heading 3,* and so on, you can use the *table of contents* facility in your program to print out a table of contents from these headings. This can be done at any level of detail you wish—for example, you might include only chapter headings and section headings, or you might also include sub-section headings. This facility automatically lists the page number on which each heading occurs. If you make any changes after generating your table of contents the page numbering may be upset, so you should remember to run the table-of-contents routine again, right at the end.

This facility can also be used to generate a *list of figures* and a *list of tables.* Just give your figure titles the style *heading 5,* and your table titles the style *heading 6.* Then ask the table-of-contents routine to run you a list of all entries of *heading 5,* and a separate list of all entries of *heading 6.*

Writing, rewriting and editing

So far, I have mentioned only the ways in which the word processor can help your *presentation*. Although these are very valuable, they are almost trivial compared with the big breakthrough that I mentioned in the previous chapter—the reuniting of the research with the writing. To do this, it is necessary that you be able to write as easily and creatively on the keyboard as you can with a ball-point pen on a piece of paper.

Three years ago I spent a period of study leave at another university, writing a book and doing the necessary research for it. Each morning I went to the government publications part of the library with an exercise book, wrote summaries of arguments, and copied data. Then I took a book or two out, and brought them back for reading at home, usually making notes of them also. (I should have entered these in *Endnote* to build up my own reference system, as discussed earlier, but at that time I didn't have a computer at home.) Finally, I went into the computer room and started writing my book. Often it was not easy. Groups of students were there, talking about their joint reports. (They should have been doing that elsewhere, or perhaps the university should have had a project area, fitted with computers, where noise and activity was to be expected. Once, libraries were completely quiet areas, but now project areas are usually set aside in them in such a way that noise from them will not disturb those who wish to read or think.) Others were printing drafts on dot-matrix printers (very noisy; fortunately quieter printers are now becoming competitive in price). But most distracting of all were the 'woodpeckers'. Students would come in with handwritten drafts and laboriously copy them on to the screen by pecking away at the keyboard with one finger of each hand.

It took me quite a while to work out why the woodpeckers bothered me so much. It wasn't the noise so much—one can learn to ignore most sounds, as long as they are not conveying a message that demands attention. That was just it: the message kept coming to me, 'You are wasting your time, and destroying your creative opportunities at the same time'. I wanted to jump to my feet and tell these complete strangers to do it another way.

The great breakthrough—writing on to the screen

When I bought my first computer in 1986 my two daughters, who were both secretaries, told me that it was essential to learn proper fingering, and to learn to touch-type. They gave me their old typing lesson books. I think they were getting their own back in this role reversal, but I followed their advice and spent tedious time learning how to do it. I commend their advice to you. Not only does this skill give you the opportunity to type faster and with less physical stress; it is also likely to help you with the great breakthrough—writing on to the screen.

If you too are a newcomer to computers, you will probably start by doing a bit of creative writing with pen and paper, as you have always done, then copy it on to the screen by typing on the keyboard. At this point you might print what you have done, and annotate the printed copy with improvements and corrections. You will then type in these alterations to produce an improved version. *Don't!* Instead, force yourself to think through your improvements on the screen, rather than on paper. Quickly you will learn the power of the standard editing devices built into the program, and you will rejoice in the clean, edited version produced immediately, without any crossings-out, insertions, arrows pointing where things are to go, and so on. I promise that, if you persist with this, in only a day or so you will suddenly say to yourself, 'I did it: I thought a whole new sentence on to the screen'. From that moment on, your life as a writer will be transformed. Quite apart from saving time and paper, and eliminating the double handling by an external party, the hired typist, you will have opened the door to the whole possibility of integrating your writing with your research, so that writing itself becomes part of the research process rather than something that happens when the research has finished.

Structure and the 'outline' view

In Chapter 2 I urged you to devise a draft structure for your thesis or report before writing anything. In Chapter 3 I suggested how you might start to write drafts of bits of the report, using this structure as a framework. Your word-processing program may have a facility to make this process much easier. The material that you type is normally scrolled continuously down the screen; if you had a long enough piece of paper to print it on, it would appear as one continuous script. This version of what you have typed is called the *normal view* (or in some programs the *galley view,* because galleys are the continuous prints produced by a typesetter before the material for a book or newspaper is broken down to fit on to pages).

Other views are available in some programs. A *page view* breaks up what you have typed into pages, complete with headers, footers, page numbers, footnotes etc. If your program has this facility, select this view, and you will see on the screen how your typed material will appear when it is printed as a report. Although this is obviously a very useful facility, you won't usually do your word processing using this view. The problem with *page view* is that it takes much more computing time to make editing changes, as they might have repercussions on other pages and the program would have to repaginate the whole document to accommodate them.

The third view that may be available to you is the *outline view.* This breaks the material down into a hierarchy of material: unindented headings (which the default settings on your style sheet will label *heading 1,* and which you might reserve for chapter headings), headings indented once (which your style sheet will label *heading 2,* and which you might reserve for section headings); headings indented twice (*heading 3,* reserved for sub-section headings), and so on—and, finally, ordinary text. When you switch from *normal view* to *outline view* you will see this hierarchy expressed very systematically by the system of indents.

Three very powerful features are built into the *outline view.*

- Simple mouse or keyboard instructions permit you to suppress as much of the hierarchy as you wish. For example, you could hide all the ordinary text and leave only the headings. Or you could hide, in addition, all the sub-section headings, leaving only the section headings and the chapter headings. Or you could hide all but the chapter headings. This feature enables you to see very clearly the structure of the report, and to identify problems such as repetitions and logic gaps.
- You can insert additional headings in response to these problems, or move sections or even chapters around to improve the logic flow. You can also promote or demote a heading to a different level in the hierarchy. You can do this after you have hidden any ordinary text to help you to see quite clearly what you are doing. But whenever you move a heading from one place to another, or promote or demote it, it takes with it all its subsidiary material that you have temporarily hidden. When you have finished all of this rearranging, you can switch back to *normal view,* and you will see that it has all been rearranged. No doubt you will then have to do some editorial work to tidy up the logic. When you have attempted this, you may find that what seemed like a good idea won't really work. Just switch back to *outline view* and reverse the whole process, or try something else.
- Your program, as we saw earlier, will have built into it a facility for producing a table of contents from material labelled with heading styles. Your outline view can give you a draft of this table of contents. You can try just chapter and section headings, or you can call up the sub-section headings also, and see whether they improve the table of contents or make it worse. (I strongly recommend that you keep to just chapter and section headings—if you can keep the table of contents to one or two pages it gives the reader a very clear map of the structure of the whole thesis or report. This will be apparent to you when you look at alternative versions using the outline view.)

File management

University lecturers have become accustomed over the years to all the standard excuses that students have invented for not submitting assignments on time. The word processor has spawned a completely new set, mostly to do with poor disk or document management. The great slave can become an obstinate enemy! If you follow a few simple rules you will avoid the most common problems.

Saving and duplicates

When you type material you are storing large amounts of information in the electronic circuitry of your computer (not in its hard disk, which I shall return to shortly). The storages consist of millions of electronic switches, each of which is in the *on* or the *off* position. As you operate the keyboard you are instructing certain switches to be turned on, and it is the pattern of *ons* and *offs* that the word-processing program interprets as letters and numbers arranged on the page. If you accidentally turn the computer off ('My dog pulled the computer's electrical lead out of the power point'), all these switches will be turned off, and the material you have typed will be lost. To store this information permanently, you have to transfer a copy of the pattern of *ons* and *offs* to a magnetized disk. This process is called *saving* to the disk. You could save to a *floppy disk* (the small portable disk that you insert in the disk slot in the machine) or into a *hard disk* built into the machine itself, which can accommodate far more material.

The first rule, then, is to save the document you are working on *frequently*. Most programs have a prompt built into them that asks you every few minutes whether you want to save now. You can set the prompt time yourself to allow the best compromise between time lost by saving too often, and information lost if you happened to lose power. Most people go for 15 minutes.

However, you should realize that when you save your document on to the disk you automatically delete the earlier version of it by overwriting it with the new version. For example, if you are playing around with extensive editing of a document called *Ch 8 Discussion* and have saved once or twice, then decide you don't like the new version after all, you will have lost the original ('Somehow I lost half the stuff on my disk'). Therefore, if you have any doubts as to whether you might want to keep the earlier version, make a copy of it and call it *Ch 8 Discussion/A* before you start editing. This is probably quite routine for you by now, but it becomes an important problem again when you start working on a joint report (see below).

Keeping a master disk

If you are like me, you have access to a computer at work, and your own computer at home. You might do some work on a document on your computer at home, then some more work on the same document on the computer at work. To do this, you will have made a copy of the document on a floppy disk to carry it from place to place. Most computer experts say that it is sound practice to build up your master document on your hard disk rather than on a floppy disk, because a hard disk is less likely to break down than a floppy disk. The floppy is then a duplicate you make of the document before you close the computer down. But this way you will end up with two separate masters on two separate hard disks, at work and at home, and the distinct possibility of overwriting a master document with the copy on the floppy disk. There are quite a few ways of dealing with this problem, but you must think them through and devise strict rules for dealing with it.

My solution is to make the floppy disk the master disk, and risk the possibility that it might break down one day ('My disk blew up'). As you will see in a moment, even if this were to happen, it would not be a big disaster. It works like this. You are about to start your thesis, and decide to start with a draft of Chapter 3: Theory. Take a floppy disk, insert it in your home computer, format it, and call it *Thesis 1*. This is your master disk. Then open a document on it and call it *Ch 3 Theory*. Immediately copy this empty document on to your hard disk, and type as much of *Ch 3 Theory* as you wish, saving every 15 minutes as you go. Before you close down for the night, copy this version of *Ch 3 Theory* from your hard disk on to your master floppy disk. You now have the latest version of your document *Ch 3 Theory* on your master disk (the floppy disk) and a copy of it on your home hard disk. This is the master document. If the floppy 'blows up' you still have the latest version of the master document at home.

You now take the master floppy disk, *Thesis 1*, to work, insert it in your work computer and copy the latest version of your master document *Ch 3 Theory* on to it. Do some more work on this document on your hard disk but, before you close down for the day, copy the latest version of it on to your master floppy disk. You now have two copies of your latest version of *Ch 3 Theory*, one on the work hard disk, and one on your master disk, the floppy. You take the floppy home, insert it in the home computer, copy *Ch 3 Theory* on to the home hard disk to overwrite the previous version, and do further work on it. Before you close down, copy this latest version of your *Ch 3 Theory* back on to the master floppy disk.

If you do not have sole control of the work computer, and therefore cannot safely leave a copy of your latest version of *Ch 3 Theory* on it, you could take a copy on a duplicate floppy. I think it better not to do this, as one day you will get the duplicate and the master tangled up with each other (in my experience this is the most common cause of the puzzled statement, 'Somehow I lost a lot of stuff on my disk').

Joint authorship

The problem I allude to above becomes critical when you are producing a joint report, with contributions from three or four authors—some with their own computers at home, others relying on computers at work. The only solution to this is to decide, fairly early in the project, that one of you will be the keeper of the master disk and the master document or documents on it.

Before anyone types a single word, the curator of the master document draws up a style sheet for the master document or documents on the master floppy disk.* Each of the partners then selects and names his or her own floppy disk, and the keeper of the master document transfers the master style sheet to each of these working disks for use on every document opened on them.

Work then proceeds as follows. The partners devise a draft outline, as discussed earlier in this chapter (this will not be easy!), then negotiate as to who will do preliminary research on various aspects of the work and write drafts reporting on this research. As draft material is produced, each partner prepares printed versions of the individual documents for discussion by the whole team, who make decisions jointly as to what changes need to be made. Alternatively, each member gives any new material to the keeper of the master document, who then pastes it into the master document, as far as possible according to the outline, to produce a draft of the complete report. The team then discusses the printed version of this draft. The keeper will also type in (in bold) problems he or she identified when attempting to fit it all together. The second method is probably more difficult, but may be more fruitful. One advantage is that it generates a new outline, which you can look at using *outline view*. Perhaps it should not be used until the whole report is starting to come together.

Whichever way it is done, it is essential that the keeper of the master be the only one to paste or type new material into

---

* If it is a relatively small report, say no more than 20 000 words, you could incorporate all of it in one document, with different chapters of the final report constituting sections of the document. For longer reports, it will be more convenient to have separate documents for each chapter.

it—of course following general agreement from the discussions of the team. The team may develop two or three options for structuring the report, and incorporate contributions from individual members into these structures in different ways, so long as it is recognized that these are not two versions of the same master document, but rather alternative master documents. Such alternatives should be given quite different names to emphasize their separate status.

5 Presentation

Good presentation is crucial to the success of your thesis or report. Everything you do in presenting it will help or hinder the reader's understanding of your argument.

Formatting of the text and choice of typeface for text and headings can help the reader to understand the structure you have used. It is my experience that the two reinforce each other, and that poor design of the format often indicates poor structure. The same is true of writing style. Turgid writing is a great barrier to understanding, and often indicates muddled thinking. Undergraduate students often view good punctuation and grammar as optional extras. When I point out errors in expression, they frequently complain that I am being 'picky', and assert that I should concentrate on what they have to say rather than on how they are saying it. But the detail obscures the substance. Having to read a sentence two or three times to work out what it is saying interrupts the flow of meaning to my brain, and has me wondering whether *they* know what they mean. Usually they don't believe me!

There are many other important small points of presentation that affect the transmission of the argument from writer to reader. Style manuals deal with these in detail. I shall not go over them here, but I urge you to obtain a copy of a good style manual, and to keep it beside you, along with your dictionary, as you write.* And whenever you have the slightest doubt about what you are doing, use one or other of these, or both. Don't just assume that what you have picked up somewhere is right; check it! You are trying to communicate, and knowledge of the meanings of words and the conventions of grammar and punctuation will assist you in this communication (see the Appendix for an introduction to two of the most important of these, punctuation and link words). If you misuse words or break the conventions (or even invent your own) you will hinder communication.

Tables, diagrams, graphs, and photographs augment the written word. Although there are many books that deal with figures and tables, they are mostly concerned with the techniques of constructing them.† I shall deal more with the relationship they bear to the written text.

Design and layout

Consistency

Should I start new chapters on a new page? Should I start new sections on a new page? Should I number sections? What typeface should I use? How should I vary it for chapter headings, section headings, sub-section headings etc.? How long should my paragraphs be? How should I indicate the start of a new paragraph? Should I use footnotes? Or endnotes? How should I reference material? How should I justify text? How do I handle quotations from the work of others? These are questions that students often ask.

---

* For Australian writers I recommend the Australian Government Publishing Service (AGPS), *Style Manual for Authors, Editors and Printers,* 5th edn, AGPS, Canberra, 1994. Many other style manuals are available, and you will find that their recommendations are similar to those of the AGPS manual.

† See, for example, L. Reynolds and D. Simmonds, *Presentation of Data in Science,* Martinus Nijhoff Publishers, The Hague, 1983.

The short answer is that you have great latitude in your choices, so long as you are consistent in what you do. Once you have established a pattern, stick to it, and the reader will get the same message ·every time. For example, main section headings, wherever they appear in your document, should always be in the same typeface, of the same size and the same character (bold, italic or whatever). They should always be preceded by the same space separation from preceding text, and always be followed by the same space separation, and should always be justified in the same way (see any style manual for definitions and techniques of justification). If the style you choose is clearly different from that for other headings, the reader will always get the message, without even having to think about it, that 'We are starting a new main section' or, 'This is a sub-section within the section'.

In the previous chapter I introduced you to style sheets. If you use them you will always be consistent, and will save time. I strongly recommend them. I can guarantee that if you use a style sheet once, you will never go back to the old way.

In practice, some conventions have developed that put some curbs on what you do. I shall go over these briefly below. You should follow these conventions, because, like word meanings, grammar and punctuation, they represent an assumed shared knowledge. I shall also give you my views on some things that I think work well, but have not yet become conventions.

Headings

Novels conventionally have chapter headings, but no section headings within chapters. Articles in newspapers have headlines, but no section headings. Why should we, therefore, have section headings and even sub-headings in reports and theses? In a novel or short story, or even a newspaper article, the writer often wishes to catch the reader unawares, and even chapter headings may be somewhat obscure. However, in a report or thesis *you want the reader to know where you are going.* Writing a thesis in such a way as to try to catch the reader unawares is a dangerous business!

Students often write page after page without a single heading. When I point out to them the need for signposting, they often reply that there are other ways of indicating where you are going and that, if the writing is good enough, headings are unnecessary. Of course, this is true, but it is a very big 'if'. Professional writers such as novelists and journalists can do it, because they *are* professionals, but professional research workers are not professional writers, even if they have been reporting their work in writing all their lives. (I might add that the students who use this argument have seldom written more than one or two sustained reports of their own work.) My experience is that perhaps one in twenty research workers can write as well as that, and that even they would be wise to put their writing to the test of seeing whether they *could* insert the headings at the appropriate places, just to check their logic flow. But it would be presumptuous of you, especially if you are early in your writing career, to imagine that you are not one of the nineteen others.

Headings should indicate where the argument is going. In a report or thesis describing an experimental investigation, chapter headings may take the quite conventional form of 'Previous theory', 'Experimental method', 'Results', 'Discussion' and so on. We might expect more descriptive section headings: for example, in the chapter on 'Experimental method' we might have the section headings 'Hypotheses to be tested', 'Selection of method', and 'Design of experiments'. In the 'Discussion' chapter we might have section headings that foreshadow the principal findings. In a paper or thesis in which a new theory or idea is being developed, as one might find in the humanities, less conventional chapter headings would be normal. Nevertheless, my broad argument still applies.

Here is a good test: if you have *outline view* in your word-processing program, use it to throw up just the chapter and section headings on the screen, without any text. Then ask yourself whether this listing would make sense to your intended readers, whether it would give them a good map of your entire report or thesis. This is a test not only of your overall structure, but of the words you have used in your headings to describe it.

What typeface should you use for headings? How much space should you leave between the previous text and the new heading? You have much freedom in this. You can design the layout in whatever way you please, *as long as you are consistent.* But there is one important convention: the design must express the hierarchy of the headings. All headings have to stand out from the text. The most important heading, the chapter heading, should stand out the most; the next, the section heading, should stand out less; and the next, the sub-section heading, less still. (A typical arrangement is to have chapter headings in bold character format, 14 or even 18 point, capitals or small capitals, and centred. Section headings are also in bold type, 12 or 14 point, again capitals or small capitals, but left-justified. Sub-headings are in 12 point bold, lower case, left-justified. Sub-sub-headings (if any) would be in 12 point, the same as the text, not bold, lower case, left-justified.)

Please don't do what Barry did. He was writing his research report for his masters-by-coursework research project, and had just been introduced to his first powerful word-processing package. It had many typefaces (Geneva, Times etc.); many type characters (bold, shadow, etc.) and, of course, many type sizes. He wanted to get the benefit of them all. In one chapter a section heading in Chicago, shadow, 14 point was followed by one in Geneva, bold, 12 point; in the next chapter a section heading in bold, Geneva, 12 point was followed by one in New York, outline, 14 point and so on. This capriciousness totally disoriented one of the examiners, and led him to fail the report (it did have other faults, but the disintegration caused by the poor design of headings completely buried its many virtues).

How many levels of heading should you have in this hierarchy? Again there are no rules, but my experience is that if you break the headings down to too many levels they become disintegrative and detract from, rather than add to, the sense of direction. The test is this: are my headings helping to structure the report and tell the reader where I am going? Chapters, sections and sub-sections should generally be enough. Very occasionally you might need one more level.

Everyone numbers chapters. Some people also like to number sections, sub-sections etc. For example, *Chapter 4: Experimental Method* might have sections *4.1 Introduction, 4.2 Hypotheses to be tested, 4.3 Selection of method, 4.4 Experimental design,* and *4.5 Conclusions. Section 4.3* might then review possible experimental approaches under *4.3.1 Participant observation, 4.3.2 Surveys, 4.3.3 Focused interviews,* and *4.3.4 Field observations.* I think you can see that it is already getting a bit fussy. If we had yet another level under *4.3.2* to give *4.3.2.1 Telephone surveys, 4.3.2.2 Postal surveys, 4.3.2.3 Shopping centre surveys,* and so on, the numbering system used to create order has, instead, resulted in disintegration. I used always to number sections, as a way of creating and maintaining the hierarchy of headings. However, word processors can do this by controlling the degree of emphasis without adding to the fussiness, as typesetters do in books. I think it is time to give up numbering systems. Perhaps in a thesis where there is much internal cross-referencing it is worth keeping one, or at the most two, levels of numbering within chapters.

Paragraphing

Paragraphing is the next level in the hierarchy of structure. A new paragraph is a signal to the reader that you have finished with one building block of your argument, and are advancing to the next one. Staying in the same paragraph indicates that you are still working on the same thought or idea.

Many writers feel uncomfortable with long paragraphs, and continually break into new paragraphs after only one or two sentences. Sometimes this is a sign that they can't really develop a thought, but in my experience it is just a bad habit—no thought is being given to what they intend the break to signify. The effect on the reader is, again, disintegration. What should come through as coherent argument appears as scrappy fragments. One-sentence paragraphs can have a strong impact on the reader—but they should be used sparingly, not habitually.

It is rarer to see the opposite fault. However, if you frequently write half-page paragraphs, either you are an expert in sustained arguments or, more likely, you are carelessly slipping from one argument to another in the middle of a paragraph. You should go back and re-read your own work, discover the points where the breaks should be, and insert them.

Type character

I have cautioned you against Barry's misuse of the wide variety of type characters now available in word-processing programs. What is their proper use? As noted earlier, you can use them to construct a hierarchy of headings, by moving progressively to less emphatic formats to represent sections inside chapters, sub-sections inside sections, and so on. You can use them to design a title page. But elsewhere you should use only two other special character formats, bold and italics.

Most programs contain underline character formats, but in my view underlining should not be used any more, as it has been superseded by bold and italic character formats. You will find my authority for saying this by opening any book. You will never find underlining in a book, because special character formats were always available to the typesetter. Because these formats were not available on typewriters, typists used underlining to make things stand out, or to indicate to a typesetter that material should be set in italics. It was always a weak substitute and, now that we have many of the tools of the typesetter available on our keyboards, we need it no longer.

How should you use italics? Any good style manual will tell you. The main uses are for titles of books and journals, for scientific names of plants and animals, for foreign phrases, and for emphasis.*

---

* The AGPS *Style Manual* cautions writers against overuse of italics for emphasis.

And what of bold character? Again, opening any book will give a good guide. Except in headings and captions to figures, bold is rarely used. Some report writers use it to give very strong emphasis. For example, recommendations made as the outcome of an argument might be in bold. Some writers scatter words in bold through their reports, together with words in italics, to indicate different degrees of emphasis. No doubt they know what they intend but, as no convention exists to tell the reader about this, it is just plain confusing. Avoid bold within text.

Writing style

Style

We all develop a writing style long before we start to write a thesis or report. Some people can effortlessly write beautiful, clear, direct English that aids communication. Others have writing styles that hinder it: verbose, ungrammatical, turgid, laboured. The strange thing is that such writers seem to be unaware of their faults, and have no desire to improve. It would take another whole book to deal with this; one I would not attempt to write. I suggest that you ask two or three people whose writing ability you respect to do you the favour of telling you what they think of your style (your supervisor may annoy you by doing this without being asked). When they tell you, don't be defensive (like my undergraduates telling me that I am being picky). Instead, thank them, and think how you might improve it. If your word-processing package has a grammar-checking routine, it might be useful to use it as one of your critics. (Mine suggested to me that I was over-using the passive voice, and I have been trying to correct this.)

I shall describe in some detail one style fault, namely *thesisese*, that seems to afflict some students. Such students have become psychologically oppressed by the problem of impressing the mythical examiners whom, they feel, will respond best to a particular form of language. It is easier to recognize thesisese than to define it. Here are two examples I encountered recently:

The initial task of the secondary assignment is to perform an analysis of locative literature; the inclusive foundation of information derived from indirect sources therefore enlightens the observational investigation of the particular landscape.

Implementation targets must be firmly established and the market and political institutional impediments identified and rigorously addressed if meaningful progress is to be made.*

Writers of thesisese nearly always use the passive voice ('targets must be firmly established . . . and impediments identified'); had the active voice been used instead ('we must firmly establish targets . . .') it would be clear who had to establish the targets and identify the impediments. Their verbs are activated by other verbs; their sentences are long and complicated; they prefer long and seldom-used words to the short equivalent words common in every-day communication; jargon is rife ('observational investigation', 'political institutional impediments'); and so on. You will see from these two examples why thesisese does *not* impress examiners. You are far more likely to impress them by using simple, direct words and sentence constructions. Remember that the university has asked them to look for critical thinking, not obfuscation.

Use of the first person

Over the last hundred years the idea developed that science was impersonal, that the scientist was a disinterested observer of the unfolding of new knowledge. It followed that scientific researchers could not claim any personal credit (or could not even display any excitement) over their discoveries when they came to report them. Theses, reports and scientific papers had to be written in the third person, as if someone else had made the discovery. Every writer knew this was nonsense, and resorted

---

* The authors of these two passages doubtless knew what they meant. I tried to convert them into simple, direct English, but couldn't, signifying that *I* didn't know what they were trying to say.

instead to use of the passive voice. So we have the wonderful downhill slide from [*first person*] 'I observed that . . .', to [*third person*] 'The researcher observed that . . .' (or if this wasn't clear enough, the incorrect, and confusing, 'This researcher [which one?] observed that . . .', or the awkward, 'The present writer observed that . . .'), to [*passive voice*] 'It was observed that . . .' (or, since the use of the passive may prevent us from knowing *who* observed, 'It was observed by the present writer that . . .'). Quite apart from using eight words where three did the job very well, we have manufactured one of the building blocks of thesisese. We have also said something quite false about science.

This tendency has never been as bad in the humanities, where people are allowed to take positions, and the first-person, active voice is permissible. Nevertheless, writers in the humanities often hide behind the anonymous third person.

When writing your thesis, what should you do? Unfortunately, most thesis examiners still belong to the old school. Rima, one of* my recent students, decided to use the first person plural in her thesis: 'We can see that . . .', meaning, 'I the writer and you the reader can see that . . .' I did not discourage her, as I thought it came up well. But one of her examiners didn't like it at all, and grumbled at her use of the 'royal' plural. Perhaps he didn't like being pushed into agreeing with what Rima was saying. Perhaps the use of the first person just bothered him.* Fortunately, he

---

* When I recounted this incident to my colleague Laurie Cosgrove, she told me that she had been struggling with this problem in her own PhD thesis, and had written quite a long appendix exploring the implications of the use of the first and third person in theses and reports. She commented that to use the first person plural was merely to avoid facing the problem, and she was not surprised that the examiner had detected this evasiveness. She believes that sometimes the first person should be used, and sometimes the third person, even in the same thesis or report—they signify different things. Evidently the problem is more complex than I had imagined. Looking back over the text of this book, I see that I have used both myself. Nevertheless, I maintain that the custom in 'scientific' writing has been to use the third person always, even when the first person is more appropriate.

was not the kind of examiner to let personal prejudices get in the way of proper appraisal, and he passed the thesis. However, I have come across the other kind of examiner too often to advise students to 'make a statement'. One of my present students, who is writing a humanities-style thesis, is experimenting with the use of the first person where appropriate. For the experimental thesis, I reluctantly counsel caution for a little longer.

Many of the learned journals now let authors use more direct forms of writing, including the first-person singular. I recently submitted an article to *Environmental Management* entirely written in the first person, describing what *I* did, what *I* thought, what *I* concluded. I did this with some hesitation, as authors contributing to this journal all seemed to use the traditional third person, but neither the referees nor the editors even commented on it. If you are writing reports or papers, I suggest you be adventurous. If the client or the editorial board object, they will soon let you know.

The 95 per cent syndrome

The 95 per cent syndrome,* although not exactly a presentation problem, has a similar effect. Let me explain. As they get further and further into their projects, students (and experienced researchers also) often fail to realize how expert they are becoming in their area. They don't realize the extent to which they have absorbed the important ideas that have dominated their particular field. When they start writing about their own research, which is about the extension and modification of these ideas, they assume that the reader will be just as familiar with the basic ideas as they are, and they don't bother to go over them. They assume the 95 per cent and concentrate on the 5 per cent.

---

* The grammar-check in my computer program reminds me that I should not use the word 'syndrome' unless the context is medical. Elsewhere it is jargon. I think the '95 per cent syndrome' *is* almost a disease, and have allowed myself the indulgence of retaining the word.

Wrong! First, very few people in the world will be as familiar as they are with the basic ideas. Who else has spent three years studying them? Second, although their readers, the examiners, may be assumed to be generally familiar with the field of the work, they will not necessarily be familiar with the fine detail of it. Quite often one examiner will be chosen because of familiarity with one aspect of the work, and the other examiner, similarly, because of another aspect. Both will be chosen more for their ability to judge critical thought in the area than for their detailed knowledge. (My own university, for example, requires that both examiners of PhD theses be attached to or associated with academic institutions.) Critical thought will include, amongst other things, clear and critical exposition of existing thought on the topic, rather than taking it for granted and hardly mentioning it.

So, don't ever assume that the examiners will know 95 per cent of what you have learnt during your project, and that you have to discuss only the 5 per cent that you believe is new and challenging.

Referencing

Referencing is the labelling of material you have drawn from other writers with enough information for the reader to be able to locate the source. You must be scrupulously careful about referencing. There are several reasons for this. First, ideas are in some way the property of the originator. If you use them without acknowledging the source, you are stealing them (the technical name for this is plagiarism). Plagiarism applies not only to a direct quote from another person's work, but also to the use of an idea put forward by another. Readers who have read the same literature as you have will probably detect your plagiarism, and will brand you a thief. Second (and this applies especially to theses), you must demonstrate that you know what you are talking about. Amongst other things, this requires you to demonstrate that you know where important ideas have come from, who have been the protagonists, what disagreements there have been, and what the present state of the argument is. This might require you to draw on the writings of many workers. You must reference all of them. Third, the reader might doubt the drift of your argument and, if you have drawn on the work of others to support or develop it, the reader must be able to go back to the originals to check for him or herself.

You may also wish to use graphical material drawn from other sources. If you use it without acknowledgement, you are stealing it, just as you are with written material. Worse, most graphical material is copyright, and you might find yourself in trouble if you do not get permission to use it.[*] It is a good rule to include in the caption of every photograph or table or figure a line saying: 'Source: Brown, 1983, p. 23'. Even if the work is your own, you should say so. For example, beneath a graph you might say: 'Source: Constructed by the author from the data of Tables 3.3 and 3.4'. Under one of your own photographs you would put: 'Source: Photograph by the author'. I was once asked to examine a thesis in an area in which I had published extensively (a not unusual circumstance). Leaping out of the page at me in the discussion chapter were several plots of my own data, photocopied straight out of an international journal but given new figure numbers, without any acknowledgement at all. Although I could see that the candidate had done this in all innocence, I could not help being annoyed. It's not a good idea to annoy examiners! Worse, the candidate was demonstrating that he had still to learn about the rules of referencing.

Several *referencing systems* are available. The most popular are the numbered note system and the name and year (Harvard) system. Any good style manual will give the rules for using these and other systems. Which reference system should you use? Most books use the numbered note system, because it is

---

[*] The same applies to direct quotes of written material, although the rules here are a little more flexible. You certainly should get permission to quote a poem or a long passage of text.

more flexible. It permits the writer not only to acknowledge sources, as discussed above, but also to make comments that are important but would interrupt the flow of argument in the text. However, over the last few decades the Harvard system has grown in popularity, and for typewritten reports and theses it has become the norm. This is because it does not use sequential reference numbers in the text—only the names of the authors and years of publication. The advantage to you as the writer is that, if a redraft of the text requires you to insert or delete references, tedious renumbering is not needed. As with so many other things, this is a difficulty associated with material prepared by typewriter. Most word-processing programs include note systems that allow for automatic renumbering of notes in this situation. Thus, the practical barrier to the use of note systems has been removed, and I foresee a swing back to the more flexible and less intrusive note system of referencing.

Figures and tables

What is the function of graphs, diagrams and photographs? Why are you using them? The immediate answer to this question is always, 'I use them when they express the point I wish to make more clearly than the written word does'. While this is true, I believe it is only part of the truth. If you wish to get the best out of your graphic material, it is necessary to put yourself in the position of the reader.

How do readers use graphic material? Do they read the written text until they get to the sentence, 'Figure 6.2 shows that increasing the population density decreases the per capita consumption of petrol', and then dutifully find Figure 6.2 to check that this is indeed so? I suggest that long before readers begin Chapter 6 they will have opened the report or thesis and skimmed through it, 'reading' the diagrams and looking at the photographs. This will trigger certain thought processes and tentatively implant certain images. There may be other preliminaries, such as looking for the aim of the research and reading the conclusions (the table of contents should permit readers to find these easily). Then the real reading begins. The written text develops ideas in the way that the writer intended, and readers will no doubt follow these. But at the same time they will be generating their own set of ideas. They will compare written text in one chapter with diagrams or text in another in ways that the writer had not intended. They might refer to and puzzle over Figure 6.2 long before the writer draws attention to it. They might return to it again when something written in Chapter 8 triggers another thought.

Reflect on the way *you* read graphic material; I am sure it will be similar. Readers use several complementary channels of communication simultaneously, some using words and some using visual images. (Other media such as theatre or television use sound channels also.) Readers do not use one at a time, switching from one to the other. Rather they use all of them simultaneously, perhaps giving one more attention than others at any given moment. Think of lectures you have been to where the lecturer has used overhead-projector slides to complement the spoken word. You are busy looking at one of the slides and thinking about it, while still listening to what is being said, when suddenly, much to your annoyance, the projector is turned off. The lecturer, already busy with the next point, didn't think it was of any more interest to you, but *you* were busy integrating it with the rest of what was going on in the lecture.

This leads us to some rules about visual material:

- Although a figure or table will nearly always be 'called up' by the written text, the reader should not have to read that part of the text to make sense of it. It should make sense by itself. You should fully explain the context in the caption, and draw attention to features you wish the reader to note, even if you have discussed these in some detail in the text.
- Try not to cram in too much detail. When I ask students their view on the functions of tables they often tell me that it

is to record data such as experimental readings in a systematic way. This being so, they argue, a table might have to contain large amounts of data, perhaps extending over several pages, and with each entry given to four or five significant figures. Such data should *not* go in the main text, but rather in an appendix. A table in the main text must be a complementary channel of communication, and large masses of undigested data will never be that. You should put a table in the main text only when the patterning obtained by arranging things in rows and columns will tell the reader something better than or different from a normal written description. If the data in your table seems to you to demonstrate some trend or correlation, you should consider displaying the trend by means of a graph in the main text, and banishing the figures to a table in an appendix.

- When demonstrating trends or correlations in a graph, think carefully about what you are trying to demonstrate. Usually you will be either confirming an established model or developing a new one, and you should have this in mind when plotting your graph.

Authors often suppress the zero point on one or both of the axes 'to make best use of the available space', or so students frequently tell me (although experienced research workers are just as guilty). Apparently this is part of the folklore of 'graphs' as learnt at school. Forget it! It is far more important to think about the trends or correlations you are trying to demonstrate than to eliminate blank spaces on your graph.*

A similar error is the introduction of an extraneous variable. I recently saw a striking example of this. The authors were trying to demonstrate that reducing the lead emissions into urban air from the combustion of petrol that

---

* This is my only point of disagreement with the AGPS *Style Manual*. Its argument seems to be based on graphs being 'visually effective'. I base my argument, rather, on whether they are effective at demonstrating the point in question.

contained lead would reduce the lead concentration in the blood of children. The data available to them were figures taken over the 5-year period 1976–80. The lead emissions had been dropping over the period in response to progressive reductions in the lead content of petrol. The writers plotted both the quantity of lead in petrol sold in major cities and the lead content of the blood of children in those cities against time in years. They suppressed the zero on both axes, and chose the scales in such a way that the two curves followed each other almost exactly, as shown in Figure 2(a), which has been reproduced from their work. The obvious (but wrong) conclusion that the unwary reader would draw is that lead in blood is proportional to lead in petrol sold, with the corollary that all that one had to worry about in a program to control lead in blood was reducing the lead emissions from burning petrol.

The authors should have plotted one against the other, without worrying about the distraction of the years in which the various values were generated, and should have refrained from suppressing the zeros, as shown in Figure 2(b). This figure shows that although lead from petrol was an important contributor to lead in blood, it was not the only one. Even if lead were to be eliminated entirely from petrol, some children might still have quite high levels of lead in their blood.

I have dealt with only a few of the rules for using graphic material, but I have done so in some detail, because authors seem to use it with so little thought. What I have said about tables and graphs applies equally to line diagrams, maps and photographs. All are part of an alternative but complementary mode of expression going on *side by side* with the written word. Think clearly about what you are trying to achieve by using the graphic material; don't clutter it with unnecessary detail; make it self-standing by full and clear captioning, including the title itself; and, as with written material, if a re-reading of your draft leads you to ask yourself why you have included it, cut it out.

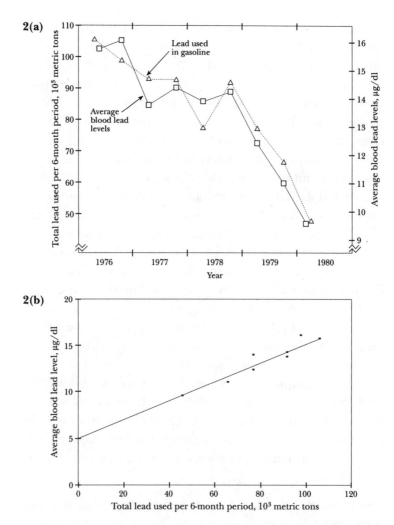

Figure 2 Different ways of expressing the relationship between lead emitted from burning petrol, and lead found in the blood of children

2(a) The year in which the measurements were taken is introduced as an extraneous variable, and the zero is suppressed for both variables.

2(b) The variables are plotted against each other, and neither zero is suppressed. This gives quite a different impression of the relationship between the variables.

Source of Figure 2(a): Committee on Advances in Assessing Human Exposure to Airborne Pollutants in *Human Exposure Assessment for Airborne Pollutants: Advances and Opportunities*, National Academy Press, Washington, 1990, p. 230.

Appendixes

Appendixes* or annexes, as we can tell from the derivation of the two words, are things appended or tacked on to the main text of a report or thesis. They do not contribute to the main argument, but have been included to support it in some way. They might establish the context of an item in the main text, or give the derivation of an equation. They are often used as a repository for raw data. They might give a sample of a completed questionnaire (in this case the main text would describe how the researcher constructed and administered the questionnaire, and would summarize the results obtained).

How do you decide what you should include in the main text, and what you should relegate to appendixes? In my own university, PhD candidates are given a word limit: theses must not exceed 100 000 words, exclusive of appendixes. Students often find that they have exceeded this limit, and the typical reaction is, 'Well, I'll have to put something in an appendix'. Although this sounds a bit arbitrary, it does make sense. The university is saying that if your argument takes more than 100 000 words, it is too diffuse, and probably you have included material that you *should* put into appendixes. But what should go? The test is quite simple: any material that would distract the reader from the argument proceeding in the main text should not be there, no matter how interesting it is, or how essential that the reader have access to it. An obvious example is the inclusion of detailed references to enable the reader to follow up material quoted from other works. It is essential that references be included in the report or thesis, but it is obvious that quoting the detail of them in the middle of the main text would be quite distracting. A list of references at the end of the report is a type of appendix. However, my test is for *excluding* material from the main text, not

---

* *Appendixes* or *appendices*? *Appendix* is a Latin word whose Latin plural is *appendices*. The modern trend to anglicize foreign plurals has caught up with *appendix*, and the Oxford dictionary now gives *appendixes* as a permitted plural. Please yourself—but be consistent.

for including it in an appendix. It might be that you should exclude it from your report altogether.

We need another test to decide what to *include* in appendixes. Paul gave me a draft chapter of his thesis to read, and it was obvious to me that, although he had put some of the material in an appendix, much of what he had left in the main text failed the first test—it interrupted the flow of his argument. I sent him off to apply this test for himself. In his revised version, with the superfluous material relegated to an appendix, the argument in the text flowed nicely. But to my astonishment I found that one of the appendixes itself had an appendix—the original appendix was now tacked on as an appendix to material that was itself now relegated to an appendix. He had written it, and couldn't let it go. Finally, perhaps to humour me, he omitted it altogether. Don't include material in appendixes unless you are fairly sure that it is necessary to support your argument. If it is a thesis, try to imagine yourself in the examiner's place and ask, 'Would I want to follow this up?' Admittedly, this is not a very strong test, but it is worth applying.

As appendixes are there to support material in the main text, you should insert a reference to them at the appropriate point in the main text. Don't include appendixes that you do not refer to in the text. (You may think that this is too obvious to mention, but I can assure you that I have often seen stand-alone appendixes.) Nevertheless, you should give the appendix an appropriate title (not just 'Appendix 3', but 'Appendix 3: Derivation of the logistic equation'), and should briefly explain its function.

6 The Introductory Chapter

I was chairman of the examination board for Graham's thesis. It was one of the most frustrating experiences I have ever had, and must have been far worse for Graham. His supervisor had suggested that he investigate a tricky applied engineering problem concerned with the flow of a particular plastic substance. As he was an excellent mathematician, he decided to look at the previous derivations of the equations governing such flow. He discovered that the standard solution given in the specialist books on the subject was a special case of a more general solution, and that generalizing this standard solution to all such flows could lead to errors. He ended up writing a brilliant thesis on applied mathematics, quite different from his original intention. *But* he had written his introductory chapter before the project took a different turn, and had neglected to rewrite it. The examiners sent the thesis back for rewriting. The introduction threw them so far off the track that they failed to realize what a brilliant piece of work he had done.

I hope this cautionary tale has impressed you. Graham had done one of the best pieces of research that I have a detailed knowledge of, but it was to no avail—he had messed up the introductory chapter.

The introduction is the shortest but the most important chapter in your thesis. It can make or break it. It has only one function: to introduce readers to the thesis. Make sure that it does this. First, tell them why the research is worth tackling—what the problem is, why it is important. End this statement of your research problem with a single sentence stating your overall research aim, which should grow out of your problem statement. You should be able to start the statement of your aim with the word 'thus' or 'therefore'. Then give a brief sketch of your research approach—how you are going to describe the achievement of it in your thesis. You should be able to start this section with the words, 'To achieve this aim, Chapter 2 does so and so . . . Then Chapter 3 does . . .', and so on.

What else should be in the introduction? My advice is not to burden it with any other functions at all: no review of the literature, no statement of theory, no glossary of terms. If you want to include these in your thesis, put them somewhere else. Make the introduction an uncluttered and absolutely clear statement of what you are attempting. If it has only three pages and other chapters have twenty pages, don't worry. They have different functions.

Problem statement

What do I mean by a problem statement? Certainly not a full review of the literature, although there might be some reference to it, because the unsatisfactory state of theory or practice might well be the problem—the justification for carrying out the work to be described. My favourite problem statement is just two paragraphs long. It is in a masters thesis written by Geoff Thomas, under my supervision, on the topic of the ignition of pulverized brown coal. This is how it reads:

> Over half the energy used in the world today is obtained from coal, mostly through the combustion of pulverized coal. Despite a great accumulation of empirical information since the first trials in 1818 very little has been discovered about the detailed mechanism of the combustion of pulverized coal.

In Victoria, the indigenous brown coal is being used to provide much of the state's energy, mostly through the combustion of pulverized brown coal in power station boilers. Although the first such trials were carried out in the 1920s no study of the fundamentals of pulverized brown coal combustion has been reported. This represents a serious gap in the knowledge required for the efficient use of pulverized brown coal.

You will note that there is no review of literature or theory here (he did do that later in his thesis), merely a simple justification that here was a very large problem that was worth putting some effort into.*

The problem statement is the context of the research, the reason it was worth tackling, the precursor to the research aim. You will have to elaborate on it later in the document, for example in the review of current theory, but not here.

Aim

Mary and two colleagues were working on a group project entitled *Coastal Management*. All from different disciplines, they conceived of 'management' in different ways. To one, it meant determining which body would have management responsibility, and how much funding would be allocated from the state budget. To another, it meant the development of management policy by the responsible body: the setting of objectives, the resolution of conflicts between potential users, and the selection of suitable management strategies. To the third, it meant detailed management in the field: the design of walking tracks and signposts, the prevention of erosion, the eradication of weeds, and so on.

---

* G. R. Thomas, Ignition of Brown Coal Particles, MEngSc thesis, University of Melbourne, 1970, p. 1. He turned out to be right. The work done by him and others who followed, using his techniques and ideas, did assist the State Electricity Commission of Victoria in designing brown coal burners by methods other than expensive, and sometimes dangerous, trial and error.

The group members could see that they were all thinking at different levels, but decided that the best way to start was for each to research the existing situation at his or her own conceptual level, and write a draft chapter on it. The supervisor of the group had previously asked them to write down the overall aim of their project, but they had great difficulty with this, as it had to accommodate the thinking at three different levels. The aim they had finally hammered out read something like this: 'To determine which body should be responsible for coastal management, how it would develop appropriate management policy, and how it would design and carry out detailed management in the field'. You will notice that the word 'management' appears in all three senses, and that there really were three different aims.

When they put the chapters together they were clearly not compatible: each member was working on a different project. The project wouldn't work until they determined which of the three levels of management was to be the subject of the investigation. They eventually decided that it was aimed at the policy level: 'To develop appropriate policy for the management of Victoria's coasts'. This did not mean that they had to throw away all the other material, but that it had to be reworked as secondary material that fed into the achievement of the main aim. For example, they would have to show how the word 'appropriate' implied some overall government view of the task and the resources that could be allocated to it, and how this affected the choice of body to carry out the task. In the problem statement, however, this material would be given a subsidiary role to the material that showed the need for policy development—imagine the difficulty they must have had in trying to write a problem statement for their initial triple aim.

You may think that the problem of multiple aims arose here solely because it was a group project. I can assure you that individual students frequently have the same problem. I have in front of me a discussion chapter for a thesis in which the student had earlier announced no fewer than four aims. Not surprisingly his discussion wouldn't work, because he was attempting to respond to all of these aims, one after the other. This completely disoriented the reader. When we analysed these aims we found that three of them were steps in the research method needed to achieve the fourth, which was the overall aim of the project. Once the student realized this, it was possible for him to deal with the findings of the first three 'aims' earlier in the thesis where they belonged, and to reserve the discussion for dealing with the real aim of the project.

Your stated aim should have three characteristics:

- It should follow as a logical consequence of the problem statement. You identify a problem; your aim is to solve it.
- It should be singular. You must identify only one aim. This is not easy to do. When I insist on this to my students they always show magnificent ingenuity in stringing all the aims they want to include into the same sentence. But three aims in the one sentence are still three aims. Inevitably you will find that some of the excess aims are in fact steps in the method that you have already subconsciously been working on to achieve that one true aim. If I were permitted to give only one piece of advice to students writing theses, it would be this: stick to just one paramount aim. If you do this, and get it right, the rest of the report will follow beautifully. If you have two aims, you will have two themes bumping along in your report together, and the reader will not be able to work out what you are doing.
- The conclusions in your last chapter must respond to this aim. Obvious? Remember Graham's thesis that the examiners sent back for rewriting, and when you have written the last sentence of your conclusions, go back and re-read your aim. If the conclusions don't respond to it, you had better rewrite it; and don't forget, you will also need to rewrite the problem statement that leads up to it.

Research approach

The research approach should follow on logically from your statement of the aim. You should be able to start it off by saying,

'To achieve this aim, Chapter 2 does . . . etc.' In other words, it is a slightly expanded version of the table of contents but, rather than writing it in the form of chapter and section headings, you should write it in the form of sentences to ensure that the logic flow is clear to the reader.

I suggest you call this small section 'Research approach', rather than 'Method', even though it describes the method that you will use for your whole research project. The difficulty is that most people use the word *method* to describe the method used in that part of the total research program that they have designed themselves—their own surveys, interviews, observations, experiments etc. They then often give Chapter 4 or 5, which introduces this research program within a research program, the heading 'Method'.* The point is that you are in danger of using the word in two senses: the method used to develop the whole of the report or thesis, and the method used for that part of the research program that you designed yourself (which I labelled *own work* in Figure 1. You must decide in which sense you will use it. I've tried it both ways, and conclude that it is best to reserve it for the method used in that part of the work designed by the researcher, and to use *research approach* to describe the approach used in the whole project—which will include historical reviews, reviews of theory and practice, accounts of the researcher's own work, and synthesis of all of these to permit conclusions to be drawn.

---

* More often the word 'methodology' is used but, as any dictionary will show, this means the science of method, or the study of method; as such, it should be avoided altogether.

7 The Background Chapters

Depending on the nature of the report, the background chapter or chapters may take many different forms. However, their function is always the same: to provide the context for your own work.

The three most common types of background material are:

- *Descriptive material* to locate study areas in space, time or culture.
- *Reviews of theory or practice.*
- *Preliminary investigations or surveys* done by you or others which will help to formulate hypotheses for the major research program to follow.

You may have one or more of these, depending on the type of research you are doing. For example, if you were reporting on strategies to control the environmental impact of human activities on Antarctica, you could easily have one of each. You would certainly need a chapter describing the Antarctic climate and landform. You would also have a chapter surveying the development of human activities there, together with the impacts of these activities. You might also include another chapter reviewing the theory of the control of environmental impacts. You could then follow these background chapters with accounts of your own surveys to establish likely future trends, and with critical thinking about how future problems might best be contained. However, none of this would make sense to the reader unless you had already laid down a background of common knowledge in the earlier background chapters.

Descriptive material

Tony McDonald was writing a research report on the effects of laser grading on irrigated farmland.* One such effect is alterations to plant growth caused by disturbance to the soil by the grading operation. To understand this, the reader needs a description of the interaction between soil, water, plants and air. How much of this should Tony have included as a background chapter? At first he left it all out, assuming the reader would know as much about this as he did (the 95 per cent syndrome that I mentioned in Chapter 5). I, his supervisor, didn't, and told him that he would have to include enough of this material so that the policy maker, as distinct from the agricultural scientist, would be able to understand what he was talking about. A week or so later I asked how his description of the soil and plants was going, and he told me that he had written about thirty pages and was only half way through. He was busily paraphrasing from half a dozen standard soil texts and distilling the thoughts of the three soil scientists he had previously interviewed! What he should have been doing (and eventually did) was something between these two extremes.

What tests should you apply to find out what to omit and what to include? I suggest two:

- Never include anything in a report or thesis that is not needed to understand what will follow. Although we need some soil science to understand the basic effects of laser grading, there is a lot that is not relevant to the problem.

---

* A. McDonald, Long and Short Term Effects of Laser Grading upon Irrigated Agricultural Land in Victoria, MLArch research report, University of Melbourne, 1989.

- Don't include anything in your main text if it is going to interrupt the development of your logic. There may be some things that have to be included in the report, but that should be in appendixes rather than the main text.

In Chapter 3 I suggested that, if you were having trouble getting started, a good chapter to start on was a descriptive chapter. You can see now the problem with this bit of advice: you are likely to include much irrelevant material because you haven't yet written the chapters that depend on the descriptive material. I still think it is good advice, but you must be ready later, when you have written these chapters, to put the knife to any unnecessary material.

Review of theory

One approach to thesis writing requires students to critically review the literature and produce a chapter entitled 'Literature review'. Usually they are not permitted to proceed with their own work until they have submitted this review, all formally typed up. The idea is that, informed by their literature review, students will be able to see just where previous workers have drawn unwarranted conclusions or have disagreed with each other, and will be able to design brilliant experiments to resolve these problems.

Certainly you should read the literature before you leap into a full-scale research program. Certainly you should learn how to follow the important arguments through, and understand the agreements and disagreements. But until you have done some work of your own it will not be possible to be 'critical' in the sense implied by 'a critical review of the literature'. It follows that you will not yet be able to design those brilliant experiments that have so far eluded all the skilled researchers in the area. You will be able to design a research program, but almost certainly it will be tentative. With luck, the results may help you to design a better set of surveys or experiments next time (by now you will have thought about it a bit more, and will have gone back and re-read the literature). It also follows that your 'review of the literature' will be an ongoing process. You will probably still be reading it when you are writing your conclusions.

I would urge that any formal literature review that you do *before* you begin your own work should *not* appear in the final thesis in that form. A formal review at an early stage of your research might well form a useful part of your development as a research worker. Certainly, reading the literature should be an important part of your research. But this is not a book about how to do research. Rather it is about how to put the results of your research into the form of a research report. If your supervisor asks you to review the literature at an early stage, that's fine, but you should view it as a document to be used as a basis for discussion between you. What we are talking about here is a review of the current theory that is to form part of your thesis. The readers are your examiners, who want to know whether you know what you are talking about. When you wrote that first review, you certainly didn't!

I have gone to some trouble to get rid of the idea that a literature review should be included as a separate chapter in your thesis. You will be referring to the literature where appropriate at nearly every point in it: in the initial review of current theory, in the approach to the design of surveys or experiments, in the discussion of the results, and in the interpretation of them to develop new theory. So why have a chapter called 'Literature review'?

What we should have, for most theses and many reports, is a *structured account of theory* current at the time you did your own work. You will be able to impose a structure on it, because by now you have finished your own work, which will have gone further than the work of others (that's why you were doing the research). You will write it with the critical perception of the worker who has now gone past this point.

In your structuring of the current theory, you should ensure that any hypotheses you have used in the design of your own experimental work emerge clearly (see Chapter 8). You should also ensure that the structure provides a firm base for the discussion of your own work (see Chapter 10). But remember that your reader does not yet know what you have found out. You must be careful not to anticipate your own findings.

Preliminary investigations

Peter came to me in some puzzlement, announcing that his experiments had failed. He was investigating a problem in the utilization of brown coal, and had designed some preliminary experiments based on hypotheses drawn from overseas work in the same field using German brown coals. What he expected to happen had not happened, and what had happened was quite unexpected. His 'experiments had failed'. I assured him that they had succeeded, not failed. He had been lucky enough to have the unexpected happen, under conditions where he was sure it had happened, because he was making careful observations. If he could work out why it might have happened, he would have far better hypotheses than when he was depending solely on the German literature.

Most research workers when tackling a new project will use a variety of methods. I remarked above that it is very difficult to establish from the literature alone what experimental work you should do, because you are an outsider listening to a debate. If you are to become a participant you will need to have some practical experience of your own. In the physical or biological sciences this might consist of designing some simple experiments to enable you to test the results or theories of earlier workers, as Peter had done. In the social sciences some preliminary surveys or interviews could be useful. Extracting published data of a number of different workers and trying to fit them to a popular theoretical model is another method.

Where should an account of this preliminary work appear in your report? If you have used it to help you to formulate hypotheses that you have called on when designing your principal research program, you could report the preliminary work as one of the background chapters. If it appears to form a major element of the principal work itself, you should set it aside for reporting later as part of the 'Design' and 'Results' chapters. If you report preliminary investigations in a background chapter, it will have to contain sections on the hypothesis used, the design of the work, the results and the conclusions drawn from them.

8 The Chapter on Design of Your Own Work

Vineeta Hoon had spent the best part of a year with the Bhotiya people of the Himalayas. These people spend their winters in villages in the foothills, and their summers in villages in the mountains themselves, growing crops and grazing their sheep in the valleys. The aim of her project was, roughly, to find whether the Bhotiya society could survive in modern India. When she began it, nobody could even tell her whether this society still did survive: the literature describing it had been written fifty or more years earlier.

She was told to head north, and try to find them! She did, equipped with the research techniques of the human geographer, and carrying with her warm clothes and useful instruments for measuring, weighing and recording. What was she going to do, if and when she found them? Live with them, go on the month-long trek to the summer villages, live with them there, observe them, talk with them, note what they did in their everyday activities, who took part in each activity, how long each took, what quantities of food and fuel they used, where it came from, and so on.

Some time after she finished this work, she came to Australia for a year as a guest of the Australian Federation of University Women, with the intention of writing her PhD thesis. That's how she came to knock on my door. Could I help her analyse the energy flows involved in Bhotiya farming? I could. I ended up supervising the writing of her whole thesis.

Her work illustrates, in an extreme form, the problem of research design. She seemed to have virtually no control over her 'experiments'; her subjects were just people going about their daily lives. What would she measure? What would she talk to them about? What mattered and what didn't, in terms of fulfilling her research aim? The physical scientist would be appalled at her inability to carry out those 'crucial experiments' always mentioned in accounts of the scientific method. Even many social scientists might be bothered by her inability to select representative subjects, and the difficulty of formulating and testing hypotheses about their thought and actions. Does this mean that she was just thrashing around blindly in her year with them, recording scraps of information at random, and was now faced with the task of making sense of these random observations, not to mention the even more difficult task of demonstrating to her examiners that she knew what she was doing?*

Your own work may be a long way in concept from Vineeta's. But even if it is the hardest of 'hard science', you will have the same problem as she did. You have to describe why you did what you did. By the time you start to describe your results you will be so familiar with them that you may have quite forgotten the struggle you went through to select an appropriate method for your investigations, or why you designed your research instruments as you did.† As a result, it is quite easy to jump

---

* Of course, she had set out with quite a clear idea of the research instruments she would use. In the field she had to adapt these instruments to the circumstances. What she had to explain to the examiners was why these were suitable instruments, and why they had to be adapted. See V. Hoon, Himalayan Transhumance and Nomadism, PhD ❚ thesis, University of Madras, 1989.

† I shall use the term 'research instruments' in this chapter to include all the techniques that physical and social scientists might use to carry out their 'own work': controlled experiments; surveys of various kinds; interviews of various kinds; participant observation; content analysis, etc.

straight from your background chapters to your results, with only a very brief section in the 'Results' chapter to cover these points. This could leave your reader mystified as to your reasoning, and thus make the results of your investigations difficult to follow. The examiner's task is to pass you if you show that you know what you are doing, and to fail you if you don't.

Your account of the design of your own investigations is the place where this virtue or failing is most obvious. What you say will depend on the type of research you are engaged in and the research methods that you have used. When designing the research, you will have used your preliminary reading and investigations to generate hypotheses or throw up research questions. Now you must identify these hypotheses or research questions and argue for them. If you have done your research properly you will have selected, from the range available, a research method appropriate for testing your hypotheses or answering your questions. In your report or thesis you should review the methods available and tell your reader why you chose your particular method of investigation. Finally, you will report on the specific design of the research instrument. If your chosen method involves using a case study, you will need to spend some time saying why you chose that particular case study, and describing it.

Generation of hypotheses

Daud came to us wishing to do a PhD. When I asked him what the aim of his project was, he replied that it was to demonstrate that development of his home country depended crucially on the adequate provision of household energy supplies. This is a hypothesis, not an aim. (An aim here might be to investigate the relationship between national development and the availability of household energy supplies.) This confusion is very common. More often than not, when I ask potential research students what the aim of their research is, they reply with a hypothesis. The confusion seems to be due to a looseness of expression amongst research workers when talking about research. Research is a complex mixture of creative and rational processes, and it is quite common to leap right into the middle of the research process with a hypothesis, and work backwards to the aim and forwards to the conclusions at the same time.* But it doesn't do to assume you know the answer before you start—you'll remember from the previous chapter Peter's conclusion that his 'experiments had failed'.

However, no matter how irrational and chancy the research is, the report of it must be argued logically and clearly. Therefore you must eliminate any confusion between *aim* and *hypothesis*. *Aim* is to do with directing something towards an object, whereas a *hypothesis* is a proposition made as a starting point for further investigation from known facts. Clearly the two words have quite different meanings, and should not be used interchangeably.

To be fair to my potential students, they were not really confusing the two things. They *were* giving me hypotheses: propositions that could be tested. They had perceived problems, and had developed hypotheses about them in their subconscious thoughts over a period of time. When the students came to see me they had not yet worked their way back from their hypotheses to their aims. They were thinking about what they could *do* in their research, rather than what they were trying to *achieve*. When I asked about their aims, perhaps not surprisingly they gave me their hypotheses.

This confusion should not worry us unless it persists. When I explain the difference, referring to the dictionary if necessary, students often reply that their aim is to 'prove' their hypothesis. This is not an aim either! Proving is what we *do* to hypotheses, at least in the sense of proving as testing (as in 'proving ground'). A hypothesis is just a device for enabling us to set up

---

* If that sounds confusing, it is because the research process *is* confusing. Read about it in Arthur Koestler's book, *The Sleepwalkers* (Penguin, Harmondsworth, 1959).

useful tests or experiments that will tell us whether we are on the right track in our quest. It is not the arrow pointing to the destination.

It follows that you should not use the word 'hypothesis' in the opening chapter. Your first mention of it should be in the chapter we are now discussing. When you do use it, stick strictly to its formal meaning. You should be able to deduce from the combination of your reading and your preliminary work that there are certain lines of thought worth following up, or worth testing by careful tests. These tests are the ones that, in the classical 'scientific method', are called crucial experiments. They will tell you without doubt whether your hypothesis has stood up or whether it has been demolished. Either way you have made progress.

Therefore, in the first section after the introduction to this chapter you should identify the ideas emerging from your background chapters that are worth following up in your own work. Whether you identify them rigorously as hypotheses for testing or as questions to be answered is a matter of taste. But you should develop them clearly and strongly, strongly enough for you to be able to select appropriate methods for testing them or following them up.

Selection of method

You have told your readers about your hypotheses or questions. Now you must tell them what methods you used to test the hypotheses or answer the questions, and why you chose them. You should first review the methods available to you, and then present reasons for selecting the methods you used. Students (and even seasoned research workers) often forget this step altogether when writing their reports. You may have used a fairly standard method used by your predecessors for testing the type of hypothesis you have put forward. You may have adopted a method suggested by colleagues or supervisors as being suitable. In both these cases you would scarcely be aware that you had *selected* a method. Or, as I suggested earlier, you might have put a lot of thought into the selection of your method, but by the time you came to report the results, you were so immersed in them that you completely overlooked the necessity to say why you chose that particular method.

But the reader cannot read your mind. No examiner is going to be kind enough to say, 'Well, I expect the candidate had good reasons for selecting that particular method'.

Study or case study?

Particular phenomena can be studied in their own right or to provide information on a broad range of similar phenomena. For example, we might study the seeding, germination and growth of the river red gum, *Eucalyptus camaldulensis,* because we wish to know how to control its environment to ensure its viability. Or we might study them because we recognize the species as being representative of a whole range of river-bank flora. If we found its development to be sensitive to the pattern of river levels over a few seasons (as indeed it is), we might then be bold enough to generalize, and suggest that this sensitivity could be expected in other riparian flora. In the second case, we have used the study of *E. camaldulensis* as a 'case study'. The structure of your thesis will be quite different for the two approaches.

Therefore, you must be clear whether you are investigating a phenomenon *in its own right* or as a *case study* from which you might later draw some generalizations. Let me give you an example. Emma Wakeham selected the topic 'Managing the Victoria Hill Mine Site in Bendigo' for her honours research report.* This is the site of a worked-out gold mine in the heart

---

* For reasons that will become apparent, her study was eventually given a quite different title. See E. Wakeham, The Mining Heritage Landscape: Our Cultural Past, Present and Future, BPD (Hons) research report, University of Melbourne, 1992.

of Bendigo—a provincial town of some 50 000 people in Victoria. This old mine site presents problems and opportunities: problems of safety and planning blight, and opportunities for preserving something of Victoria's mining heritage, perhaps combining this with tourism.

Emma's original intention was to investigate the management problems and opportunities in much the same way as a consultant might: to work through them in the light of existing legislation and land-use controls, and present a management plan. As her work continued, it became clear that the Victoria Hill mine site was not unique. Similar problems and opportunities were present in other mine sites, and her conclusions might be applicable to them also. Emma had slipped into considering Victoria Hill as a case study that could help her in a broader study of how to manage worked-out mines, rather than a study of how to manage Victoria Hill itself.

This almost imperceptible shift during a research project is quite common. Usually the research method doesn't have to change much, at least in the early stages, to adapt to the shift, but the report must be structured quite differently. The danger is that, because the shift *is* imperceptible, the researcher might fail to adapt the structure appropriately. In Figure 3 on page 80 I illustrate the differences in report structure, using the Victoria Hill study as an example. I wrote these two report structures without doing the research. Had I done it, I am sure that the structures would have been modified and improved. However, I don't think that the principal elements and sequencing would have changed much.

The two structures are clearly very different. The common elements appear at different points. For example, the words 'Victoria Hill' are not even mentioned in the title or the aim in the case-study approach, and the description of the Victoria Hill mine area is deferred for several chapters. The case-study investigation is far more ambitious and involves far more work. Not surprisingly, the discussion and conclusions take a quite different course.

Study of Victoria Hill alone	Victoria Hill as a case study
Title: Managing the Victoria Hill Mine Site	**Title:** The Mining Heritage Landscape: Our Cultural Past, Present and Future
Aim: To develop a management plan for the Victoria Hill mine site in Bendigo.	**Aim:** To develop principles for managing worked-out mine sites close to urban areas.
Background: Describe Victoria Hill mine site. Review legislation and land-use controls, specifically as they apply to Victoria Hill.	**Background:** Review legislation and land-use controls. Review present practice in Australia and elsewhere on rehabilitation of disturbed landscapes. Review theory of industrial heritage.
Method: Hypothesis is that contributions from several disciplines will be needed. Interview professionals such as City Planner for Bendigo, landscape architects, tourism planners.	**Method:** Hypothesis is that the management problem can be generalized. Second hypothesis is that present management is *ad hoc*, and that management principles don't exist. Select case-study method for developing management principles. Select Victoria Hill as case study.
Results: List problems and opportunities at Victoria Hill.	**Results:** Describe Victoria Hill mine site. List problems and opportunities. Review present management practice. Confirm (most likely) that principles do not exist.
Discussion: Derive and justify a management plan for Victoria Hill.	**Discussion:** Develop management principles applicable to Victoria Hill. Generalize them. Establish changes to laws and regulations required to put them into practice.
Conclusions: Summarize management plan (note that this is not really a conclusion, as this type of investigation has an outcome, rather than a conclusion).	**Conclusions:** General management principles can be enunciated. They follow a particular pattern (summarized here). Present management is inadequate. Laws and regulations should be changed (as summarized here) to encourage implementation of principles.

Figure 3 Differing report structures for an individual study and a case study

You must, then, be quite clear about which of the two approaches you are using. If you are undecided, you will jump from one structure to the other as the report develops. When you finally get to the discussion you will be in a big mess. I have seen this happen often. I can offer an excellent test: if you mention the words 'case study' in your thesis, you should not be mentioning the specific area or topic of the case study in your aim or title. If you find that it keeps creeping back into the aim or title, you have not yet sorted out this problem.

Figure 3 demonstrates that there is a leap of faith in the discussion and conclusions sections of the case-study approach, in that it is assumed that the findings for the case study can be generalized. (If you don't go on to at least some generalization, then it is not a case study, but merely a study.) You will have done your best to cover this point in your method section, in which you try to choose the most representative case-study area. However, inevitably you will spend so much time developing ideas around your case-study area that you will have little time for the even more important task of seeing how far you can generalize them. This doubt can be resolved only by checking your conclusions on several other areas, either by doing further work yourself, which you may not have time to do, or by finding reports of comparable work in the literature. Therefore, most case-study investigations leave many unanswered questions and pose many hypotheses for further research.

Thus, a case study is really only a preliminary investigation; it is a method for generating hypotheses rather than for drawing conclusions. Yet in the structure shown in Figure 3 the case study is the main investigation. This is quite valid. I know of quite a few PhD theses taken up principally by case-study investigations that have impressed the examiners enough to be passed. However, I would advise you to express the appropriate reservations about the degree to which they can be generalized, and to point out the need for further work to confirm your conclusions.

Design of research instruments

You have told the reader what research method you used and why you chose it. Before you describe the results obtained by using this method, you must first describe in detail *the way you applied the method, and why*. Two examples should help, one from the physical sciences and one from the social sciences.

Example 1 is Geoff Thomas's study of the ignition of brown coal particles that I mentioned in Chapter 6. His aim was to establish how brown coal particles ignited in burners in a power-station boiler fired with brown coal. Coal for these burners is pulverized in a hammer mill to a size range of 10–1000 microns. The pulverized coal is suspended in a stream of air or gas, mixed with the combustion air, and injected continuously into the hot flame formed by the combustion of the coal which immediately preceded it into the combustion chamber. If the coal particles do not get hot enough they will not ignite, and the flame will go out.

It is difficult to work out how the particles are igniting, for two reasons. First, the ignition process occurs very rapidly. Second, it is difficult to observe individual particles, because they are travelling at great speed and are accompanied by many thousands of other particles. Geoff decided to use an experimental method that would simulate the ignition and combustion process, but in such a way that he could observe what was happening to individual particles. In his apparatus, coal particles were glued to the end of a glass fibre using a non-combustible glue, and plunged into a stream of hot gases whose composition and temperature could be controlled. As the particles ignited, the light they emitted was detected by a light-sensitive cell, the output of which was recorded against time on a cathode-ray oscilloscope. In a variant of this procedure the igniting particles were photographed by a high-speed movie camera.

You will notice that Geoff invoked no 'hypothesis' in the selection of the method beyond the somewhat fuzzy one that if he could 'capture' the ignition process for individual coal particles he would find out something useful about the ignition of a cloud of particles.

However, the detailed design of the experiments, and hence the physical design of the apparatus, required quite precise hypotheses. The literature on the ignition of coal particles suggested that important factors were the temperature and composition of the gases encountered by the fresh coal particles, the size of the particles, the type of coal, and its moisture content. Each of these formed a hypothesis: that the temperature of the gas affected the ignition process, that the moisture and oxygen content of the gas both affected the ignition process—and so on.

He selected values of these variables over a wide range, limited only by the design of the apparatus (for example, it was not possible to glue particles smaller than 100 microns to the glass fibre), and by the practical limits of what was being simulated (for example, it was pointless to test the effect of using an atmosphere of pure oxygen, as this would never be encountered in practice). He then devised a set of experiments using the many different combinations of these levels of the controlled variables. Each combination was repeated ten times, to take account of the heterogeneity in individual coal particles. The individual experiments were performed in random order, so that no bias would occur through such factors as improvement in experimental technique over time.

In his chapter on 'Experimental design' Geoff described the general method and its limitations, the hypotheses concerning the effects of various factors, the design of experiments to test these hypotheses, and the design of apparatus to carry out these experiments.

Example 2 is from the social sciences. For his honours project Gerard Mutimer decided to study the gap between knowledge and action in the recycling of household wastes.* His idea was

---

* G. Mutimer, Environmental Attitudes and Behaviour, BPD (Hons) research report, University of Melbourne, 1991.

that if the reasons for the gap were known, it would help municipal councils to devise better recycling programs. This is a typical case of starting off with a hypothesis—that there was a gap. Clearly his project would be in great trouble if he did not test this hypothesis. Equally clearly, the testing of this hypothesis was not the aim of the project, but a step in the method.

As Gerard read the literature on the psychology of knowledge and action he realized that such a gap was a common phenomenon in many aspects of life—not just in the environmental area, and certainly not just in recycling. He decided to broaden his study to the whole environmental area, using recycling as a case study. We see again the shift from a particular study to a more general one, similar to that discussed above for the Victoria Hill mine site. This required minor adjustment to his research program, and major adjustment to the structure of the report.

His major hypothesis, then, was that there was a gap between environmental knowledge and action. His reading of the psychology literature helped him to generate a second hypothesis: that this gap was due to factors that intervened to prevent people from translating knowledge into action. The reading enabled him to categorize these factors under the headings of 'opportunities and constraints', 'social norms', 'personal rewards', and 'perceptions'.

Gerard decided that the most fruitful method of attack was to survey representative people in order to test his two hypotheses. Because of constraints of time and other resources, it could not be too ambitious. First, he had to decide how to choose his sample of people to be surveyed (by telephone, mail, knocking on doors, or stopping people on the street or in shopping centres); and what type of survey would be most suitable (questionnaire, focussed interview, observation of people's actions etc.). He decided on a 'shopping centre' survey, and chose a questionnaire as his survey instrument. He divided the questions into three parts. The first part asked formal questions about the respondent's recycling actions. The second part was aimed at the identification of intervening factors; the questions were designed to test sub-hypotheses on specific intervening factors. The third part was less formal, with open-ended questions designed to elicit the person's own perception of his or her environmental awareness, and the interviewer's assessment of that awareness. This design permitted the researcher to check whether there was a gap between knowledge and action, and to test, by cross checking of answers to the different parts of the questionnaire, which intervening factors were important.

His chapter on 'Method' had one section in which he identified his hypotheses; another section in which he chose surveys as the method to test his hypotheses and justified his choice; another on the choice of questionnaire as survey method, including the type of survey; and another on the design of the questionnaire and the reasons for the design. He had to be careful to acknowledge the problems caused by lack of resources (small and possibly unrepresentative samples), and to describe the steps he took to minimize their effects.

I have gone into these two examples in some detail, as it is my experience that this chapter is most likely to receive insufficient attention. Although the two projects used quite different methods, the points dealt with are quite similar:

- Clear identification of hypotheses.
- Explicit choice of method.
- Design of research instruments to test hypotheses.

A problem can sometimes arise if you follow this sequence. It may be that your review of available research methods has led you to select two (or even more) methods instead of one—different approaches to the same problem that are in some way complementary. If you describe the design of the research instruments straight after the selection of the methods, as I have recommended, you will have the design of two different sets of instruments in this chapter, followed by the results of the two sets of work in the next. This will disrupt the logic flow.

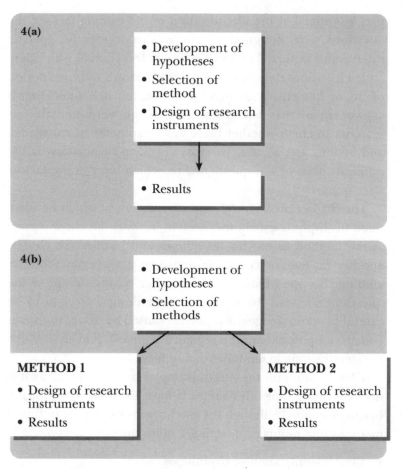

Figure 4 Design and reporting of your own work (each box represents a separate chapter of your thesis)

4(a) The arrangement of material when only one method is used.
4(b) The arrangement when more than one method is used.

If this happens, stop the method chapter at the point where you have selected the two methods, and follow with *two* results chapters instead of one. In the first you will describe the design of the first set of research instruments using the first method, followed by the results from this work. In the next chapter you will describe the design of the second set of research instruments, followed by the results from this second set of work. The difference between these two approaches is shown in Figure 4. Vineeta Hoon used this approach in her study of the Bhotiyas— one chapter on time analysis, one on space analysis, one on energy analysis, and one reporting focussed interviews—and it worked well.

9 The Results Chapter

When Professor Henry Nix, Director of the Centre for Resource and Environmental Studies of the Australian National University, gave an address on 'Environmental Data' at a seminar on environmental research in Canberra in 1992, he started off by quoting the dictum: 'Data is not information, information is not knowledge, and knowledge is not wisdom'. This impressed me so much that it has stuck in my mind ever since. I shall use it here to provide a framework for the reporting of the results of any research or investigation.

Data is the outcome of the recording of measurements or images. These data could be recorded by you as the researcher using the research instruments you devised to test your hypotheses, or by someone else on the speculation that they might be useful to somebody, somewhere, sometime. An example of the second type would be daily temperature measurements recorded at a meteorological station.

As soon as you use data to test a hypothesis it starts to become *information* (what the data tells us). Temperature data collected by the meteorological bureau becomes information when you use it in conjunction with your records of plant growth to test the hypothesis that plants grow faster at higher temperatures. Similarly, the data that you collected using your research instruments will become information as soon as you use it to test the hypotheses you used to design the instruments.

Information becomes *knowledge* when you are starting to draw conclusions from it: that plants do grow more vigorously at higher temperatures, or that the hypotheses you put forward are sustained or rejected.

Knowledge does not become *wisdom* until it is integrated into your whole way of looking at things. It is the implications of the conclusions you draw from your results that become wisdom: new insights, new theory, new paradigms.

This analysis shows us what you should include in the results chapter and what you should leave out. Raw data that does not make sense unless you explain it or display it in a suitable way should be left in the filing cabinet or relegated to appendixes. Data displayed in the form of tables or figures that enable you and the reader to make sense of it becomes information, and should be included. You will be able to draw some general conclusions from an examination of this information. This may go beyond the individual sub-hypotheses that you put forward, to interactions between the variables that you may not have expected and, if you are lucky, to some totally unexpected and quite exciting results.

You and the reader now know something that you did not know before you carried out your own work. You have stepped out of the information square into the knowledge square. At this point, stop. Keep your theorizing about this for your 'Discussion' chapter, for it is there that you advance from knowledge to wisdom.

Presenting the results

In the previous chapter of your report you described the design of the work that you were undertaking to test your hypotheses or answer your research questions. You now have to present the results you obtained in this work.

This presentation should not be haphazard. The presentation should *inform* the reader. You may believe that you should include every single figure or every bit of data that you recorded in your work. This is often very difficult because of the sheer mass of data, and is nearly always counterproductive. Consider, for example, Gerard's very modest survey on recycling mentioned in Chapter 8. This included the answers to about 50 questions put to 40 respondents, or 2000 bits of data. Analysis of the results permitted cross-correlations between answers; indeed the method selected depended on examining these cross-correlations. However, had all possible cross-correlations been included, we would have many thousand more bits of data.

Or consider Tony McDonald's work on laser grading mentioned in Chapter 7. This included focussed interviews, lasting about one hour each, with three farmers and several professionals in the area of land management. All were tape-recorded and transcripts of them prepared. Should Tony have spent so much time preparing transcripts? (It was all data.) Having prepared them, should he have included them in his research report? If so, where—in this chapter, or relegated to an appendix?

There is a clear set of rules to be followed here:

- Record and file *all* your data in a systematic way.
- In your report, offer your reader the opportunity of examining these data by private arrangement.
- Include enough of the data in an appendix for the reader to see how you collected it, what form it took, and how you treated it in the process of condensing it for presentation in the results chapter.

    For example, Tony in the end included in an appendix the transcript of one focussed interview so that the reader could see what relationship the summary of all the interviews appearing in the results chapter bore to individual interviews.
- Present your results in the chapter itself in such a way that it is clear how they relate to the hypotheses.

For example, in his study of the ignition of brown coal particles, Geoff Thomas tested 96 combinations of experimental conditions, with 10 particles tested at each combination, giving results for 960 particles in all—a formidable presentation task. First he averaged the ignition times of the group of 10 particles, and gave the standard deviation to indicate the variability from particle to particle, thus cutting down the entries in the table from 960 to 96.* Although he had performed the experiments in random order, he entered the results in the table in a systematic order. He presented all the results for 1000 micron particles first, then 500 microns and so on. He then arranged the results for each particle size in groups for each of the other variables. The reader could then examine the results with the hypotheses in mind, and develop mental pictures of the effects of the different variables. Geoff could have gone on to plot some of these effects as graphs, but he preferred to wait until the next chapter to do this, because he wished to plot the results against what he would have expected from a theoretical model he had developed earlier in the thesis.

Analysing the results

Having presented the data in an informative way, how much further should you go? In the work I have just quoted, Geoff made some general remarks about his observations before he tabulated the results. The chapter stopped abruptly at the end of the tables. He had a good reason for doing this but, as I look back on the work twenty years later, I find it a bit unsatisfying. He had some strong hypotheses to test. He had designed experiments to test them, and had carried out the experiments. Were the hypotheses upheld or rejected? The reader wants to know what the findings are before the writer goes on to discuss their implications.

---

* If he had tabulated the results for all 960 particles the reader would have had more data but less information.

In complex situations such as the above, in which there is considerable interplay of the effects of the different variables, it may not be easy to disentangle the results and their implications. Nevertheless, I recommend that you try—plot the results in terms of the hypotheses. Geoff could have plotted ignition times (a dependent variable) against the moisture content of the particles (an independent variable), with all other independent variables held constant, or against the size of the particles, or the oxygen content of the gas, or its temperature. He did these plots for his own information; but he decided not to present them as part of the results chapter because he had found that the interpretation of the results was not as straightforward as his original hypotheses indicated. In retrospect I believe the reader would have been in a better position to go on to the discussion chapter had he presented the results as tests of his hypotheses by plotting dependent variables versus independent variables. Then, in a very brief discussion, he could have pointed out the unexpected complexity, and announced that he would be dealing with this in his next chapter.

Drawing conclusions

My dissatisfaction with Geoff's chapter on results was due to its unfinished nature. Hypotheses had been tested, but we did not know what had happened. An aim had been stated at the beginning of the chapter (to report the results of experiments to test hypotheses), but it had been only partially fulfilled.

If you turn back to Chapter 2, in which the structure of chapters is discussed, you will see how important it is that you state the purpose of the chapter in the introduction, and that you write a conclusion in which you describe how that purpose has been fulfilled. This rule is as important for the results chapter as for any other. At the end of the chapter, you should share with your readers your understanding of what is now known that was not known when the chapter began. You will then have transformed information into knowledge.

10 The Discussion

Ian Nuberg had reached the discussion chapter of his thesis, and we were talking about how he might shape it. The aim of his PhD project was to determine whether agroforestry could make a worthwhile contribution to the rehabilitation of degraded tropical uplands.* He had spent a year on field research in Sri Lanka, in much the same spirit as Vineeta Hoon's work amongst the Bhotiyas (see Chapter 8), although he at least knew where he would find the degraded tropical uplands. But, like her, he had to adapt his research methods to accord with what he found around him.

In the end, he carried out two major research programs: a comparative study of existing land uses, and an economic analysis of a particular agroforestry system sponsored by a German aid agency. He had written chapters of his thesis describing these, as well as the appropriate background chapters, but now found himself in trouble trying to pull it all together. I asked him whether he knew what the overall conclusions of his research project were. 'More or less', he replied. 'Enough to write them all down?' 'Yes'.

---

* Agroforestry is the integration of tree crops, annual crops and/or animal production in the one farming system to benefit from the ecological and economic interactions between them.

The task of the discussion chapter is to take the thesis from the point where theory has been reviewed and the results of experiments or surveys reported, to the point where conclusions can be drawn as to the outcome of the whole research project. Once Ian realized that he knew what he had concluded (more or less!), the task of writing the discussion that enabled him to get to these conclusions suddenly seemed less formidable.

I shall suggest a method for tackling the discussion chapter that turns it into a relatively easy chapter to write, rather than the most difficult. For a few years now I have been encouraging my students to use this method, and it has worked for them.[*]

The task of the chapter

Why does the discussion chapter worry students so much? I think the reason is a variation on the problem I tackled in Chapter 3, that of the tension between the creative and the rational parts of our brains. In the discussion chapter the creative part of our brain is paramount, because we still have to compare the results of our own work with what we might have expected from existing theory to see what new ideas will emerge. Starting to write is, therefore, stepping into the void. I have often seen people start their discussion in this way; they thrash around with a hodge-podge of undifferentiated thoughts in their heads, hoping that something will turn up. Yet we know that we must argue the discussion very tightly to convince the reader that the conclusions we draw at the end of the thesis are sustainable. This tension must be resolved.

I advocated in Chapter 3 that you resolve this tension by composing a rational structure for the thesis that will get you logically from the aim to the conclusions. Once this structure is in place, you then start to flesh the argument out, giving the creative part

---

[*] It worked for Ian. See I. K. Nuberg, Appropriate Interventions for Rehabilitating Degraded Tropical Uplands, PhD thesis, University of Melbourne, 1993.

of your brain free rein. Your writing might require that you modify the structure, or you might leave the structure intact and modify the argument. You have set up a fruitful dialectic.

You can use exactly the same technique when writing individual chapters. Each chapter must have an aim and conclusions, and you must structure the chapter in such a way as to get you logically from the aim to the conclusions. In most chapters it is not too difficult to do this, because you know what the conclusions are before you start to write. However, in this chapter research is still going on, so you're not sure what the conclusions are. Therefore you can't design a structure that will enable you to reach them.

Structuring the discussion

How are you to design a structure for the discussion that will enable you to get logically to your conclusions when you don't know what they are? Indeed, if you had *no idea* what the conclusions were, it would not be possible.

The resolution of the paradox is simple—we are asking the wrong question. When we assume that we don't know what the conclusions are, we are only partly right. The rational part of our brain is telling us that we don't know what the conclusions are because it knows that it is the function of the discussion to *find out* what they are. But the creative part of our brain has been working on this problem ever since the research project began. It has been trying out ideas and associations, sometimes accepting, sometimes rejecting, sometimes getting it right, sometimes wrong, but seldom informing the rational part of our brain what it has been doing, or where it has got to. Without this, research would not be possible. We have been doing research in our subconscious, creative minds all the time, and we have reached subconscious, creative conclusions. (Ian knew, more or less, what his conclusions were.)

The key to writing the discussion is for you to bring these subconscious conclusions to the conscious realm, and commit them to screen or paper. Your rational brain can then sort them out and do its best to make sense of them. You can then use them to design the structure of the chapter on the assumption that they *are* the conclusions. This is how to do it:

- Write down all the things that you know now that you didn't know when you started the research; a single sentence for each item. These can be big ideas, little ideas, snippets of knowledge, insights, answers to questions, etc. Don't worry whether you are responding to the aim you set yourself in your introductory chapter. That would be a rational approach, whereas you are engaged in a process of dredging up subconscious conclusions. Consider asking your supervisor or a colleague who is familiar with your work to sit down with you while you are listing these conclusions. The presence of another person, chipping in and asking questions, may help you to uncover your hidden thoughts. You will end up with a totally undifferentiated list of twenty or thirty 'conclusions'.

- Sort these into groups of associated ideas (now using your rational brain). My experience is that you will end up with three or four groups. If you have more than four groups, you may have included conclusions that emerged earlier as conclusions to your background chapters, but which have not interacted with your own work. These probably were important at the time, but they are not conclusions from your whole research. You may test this by asking, 'Does this conclusion respond to the aim I stated in my introductory chapter?' Reject those that don't, but first check that you did give them clearly as conclusions in the earlier chapters where they belonged. If you still have more than four groups of conclusions, try coalescing one or more groups to get down to three or four.

- Give a heading to each group. These headings will form the section headings in your discussion chapter. The function of each section is to argue for the conclusions that you will be drawing later. You will have to examine these headings to see which order they should go in. (You will find that some of the groups of conclusions don't make too much sense unless you have already dealt with others.)

- Each section will contain several points, as identified by the separate conclusions that you have already listed for that section. These could form sub-headings within the section. Sort these sub-headings into a logical order, reject ones that are obviously irrelevant, add others that you now see you missed by your earlier haphazard identification process, and coalesce points under one heading if this makes sense (you should not have more than three sub-headings within a section).

You will now have a tentative structure for the discussion chapter. You may now give your creative brain leave to write the text, using this structure as a framework. When you start to write, you will not be stepping out into the void.

This balancing of the rational and creative parts of our brains by writing creatively to a rational structure will work only if you treat it as a dialectic. There will be a constant tug-of-war. Often your creative mind will take you away from the rational structure. When this happens, don't assume that the creative mind is always right. Similarly, don't assume that the rational mind is always right. But you cannot leave it un-resolved: you must bring either the structure or the wayward text into line. This problem will be particularly acute in this chapter, because the rational structure you are using is tentative, being itself based on conclusions garnered from the creative mind. However, my experience is that at this stage óf the research the creative mind has already done marvellous things, and usually you won't have to change the structure much, even though you may modify some of the individual conclusions.

The process I have described probably seems messy, with much experimentation and correction to do. Messy it is, but this is the chapter where research is still going on; it is the only one in which the act of writing might cause you to find out more, where knowledge might become wisdom. Research is a messy process. But I still maintain that you will find it relatively easy to write the chapter because you won't have to worry about what to put in and what to leave out, as you did in other chapters. This chapter is the one that all the others were leading to.

11 The Conclusions

You stated the aim of the research project in your first chapter. These conclusions must indicate how you fulfilled that aim. They also must arise inescapably from the argument in the discussion chapter. I have often seen students, and even experienced research workers, drawing conclusions that they had failed to argue for. They had argued for them in their subconscious minds but, because they did not follow a process such as the one I described in the previous chapter for structuring the discussion, they had omitted to back them up in their writing.

It is essential to forge the links between the 'Introduction' and the 'Conclusions', and between the 'Discussion' and the 'Conclusions'. As these are the conclusions to the 'Discussion', it follows that the discussion chapter does not need its own separate conclusions. You could roll these last two chapters into one, giving it the title 'Discussion and Conclusions'. This is often done in papers for learned journals. Alternatively, you could warn the reader in the introduction to the discussion chapter that you will not be drawing formal conclusions to the chapter, but will reserve your conclusions for the last chapter.

Structuring the conclusions

If you followed the suggestion I made in the last chapter you will have a set of conclusions that emerged out of each section of your discussion, rather than the ones that you dredged out of your subconscious when you started the procedure. You can now write these down as the conclusions to your research, knowing that you have argued rigorously for all of them, and that you have got them in perspective through your argument. Also, if you put them down in the order in which they emerged in the discussion, they will be in a logical order, because you arranged the discussion in a logical order.

You should now have a deep sense of satisfaction about the whole thesis! Any residual doubts will indicate that something is wrong earlier in the thesis, and you should try to find out what it is. In the next section I provide some diagnostics.

Rules about the conclusions

- I have already hinted at my first rule. If the discussion chapter is where you draw together everything you have done in your whole research project (not just your own experiments or surveys, but also your reviews and analyses of the work of others), then *you should draw your conclusions solely from the discussion chapter.* If you find yourself wishing to include conclusions from earlier chapters that you have not worked over in the discussion, you have either omitted something important from the discussion or, more likely, you are still hankering after more than one aim. That is why I said in the introduction to this chapter that you would be wise to have no conclusions for the discussion chapter other than the conclusions chapter itself.
- *There should be no further discussion in the conclusions chapter.* If you find yourself wanting to engage in further discussion, and even still quoting from the literature, you should have incorporated this material in your discussion chapter (again

it is more than likely that you have more than one aim; you have satisfied one of your aims in the discussion, but you still have another aim to deal with).

- *The conclusions should respond to the aim stated in the first chapter.* If you take your problem statement and then the aim from your 'Introduction', and follow these with your 'Conclusions', the result should be a mini-document that reads logically. If I am reading a paper, examining a thesis or report, or looking at the first draft of a thesis, I always put what I am reading to this test. It often reveals that the writer omitted to state the aim, and it is only when one reads the conclusions at the end that one can start to deduce what the unstated aim must have been.

- *Summaries are not conclusions.* I drew this distinction in Chapter 2 when talking about conclusions to individual chapters. It was important there; it is even more important here. I will repeat what I said then. Summaries are a brief account of what you found out; conclusions are a statement of the significance of what you found out—what you concluded from it. If you are merely summarizing the argument developed in your discussion chapter, you will feel quite unhappy with your conclusions. There will be no sense of closure. Also, you will almost certainly have failed to respond to the aim of the whole project. (Sometimes this happens when the aim is too modest, or even woolly. For example, when researchers say that their aim is to investigate the properties of a system, they may end up with a list of properties, a summary. This is hardly research.)

- *Conclusions should be crisp and concise.* The conclusions chapter may be only two or three pages long—which helps to give the sense of closure that I mentioned above.

12 Finishing

You have just typed the last full stop on the last of your conclusions. Finished at last! Wrong—if it is a thesis or a substantial report, you still have several weeks of work to do. You have two major tasks ahead of you:

- What you have actually finished is your first draft: a collection of chapters written according to the structure you devised. Each chapter seems coherent in itself, but you now have to consider whether the whole thing hangs together; whether your argument really gets you from the aim to the conclusions; whether your aim itself has drifted during the course of the research and writing without your noticing it; whether there is extraneous material that you should transfer to appendixes; and whether important insights have emerged to which you gave little or no prominence in your original structure, but which are now demanding more attention. When you have put all these things right, you will have finished the second draft.
- When you have finished the second draft, you still have to check all the details: format, spelling, punctuation, captions to figures and tables, references etc. Although these things are not intellectually demanding you have to do them properly, and they take time.

From first to second draft

When my postgraduate students have typed that last full stop, they usually print out clean copies of the latest versions of all the chapters straight away, put them in a binder, and give the whole thing to me for a little light weekend reading. This is not a good idea. I suggest that you have a go at revising your first draft yourself before giving it to your supervisor, not only because it is a unique and necessary experience, but also because the comment you get back from your supervisor about a document that is in good shape will be more useful than the comment about one that is still full of problems.

What I do with the first draft is parallel to what I expect the examiner of a thesis or the reader of a report would do, or what I would do if I were refereeing a paper submitted to a conference or a learned journal. The only difference is that, because I am your supervisor, I am now fairly familiar with the drift of your argument and with the approach you have taken, and I have to guard against reading things into the draft that you have not clearly explained. When you are reading your own work, this is even more of a problem. For that reason, you should put it aside for a few days before you read it as a whole.

Structure

First, I look at the overall structure. There should be a table of contents which corresponds with the chapter titles and main section headings in the text. (If you have reworked some chapters, you may have changed headings and forgotten to change them in the table of contents. If you generate a table of contents from the finished document using a style sheet, this cannot occur.)

The table of contents should tell me straight away whether there are any major logic problems. If it is not informative enough, I go to the beginning of each chapter and read the introductions in order. This will probably help, but it may reveal that the introductions themselves are inadequate. If they are, I note this in red ink in the margin of the hard copy.

Finally, I read the introductory chapter *as if I were a reader seeing it for the first time*. I ask myself: Is this telling me (the uninformed reader) why the work is being done? Is it clear what the aim of the work is? Is there an adequate sketch of how the writer intends to achieve this aim? Again, if any of these is inadequate, I note the problem in the margin. Then I go straight to the conclusions, and ask myself whether they respond to the stated aim. If they don't, I note the disparity.

The main text

Next, I read the whole draft from beginning to end, noting spelling, grammar and typographical errors in red ink as I go, and also noting things such as obscurities, patches of purple prose, and places where the argument seems to have logic gaps. At the end of each chapter I write a few lines about how the chapter shaped up in the context of everything that preceded it. The conclusions to the chapter are particularly important here. One of my commonest comments on them is that the author is still writing summaries of the chapter, rather than giving me, the reader, a sense of how the chapter is advancing my comprehension of the argument in the whole document.

By the time I have reached the end, a sense of the integrity (or lack of it) of the whole document has usually built up. If there is a problem, it may be obvious. If it is not obvious, I repeat the first step—the examination of structure—but now with a knowledge of how the whole argument has developed (or has failed to). There may be major gaps in the argument; there may be material present that is not part of the argument and that should be relegated to appendixes; there may be repetitions that should be eliminated or consolidated; there may be material that would have been better located elsewhere in the document; there may be conclusions emerging strongly at the end that the author should have emphasized more, or had failed to argue for in the discussion; and so on. Before handing it back to the author, I write a few pages on these larger problems.

Thus the author now has two sets of comments: detailed comments in the text on points of grammar and expression; and general comments about the structure of the argument. We discuss the latter, and the author gets to work on the second draft. As the author produces revisions of various parts, aimed at solving particular problems, we discuss them. I usually find that a complete re-reading of the second draft will not be necessary until after the second, more detailed, part of the finishing process that I am about to describe.

Dotting the 'i's and crossing the 't's

The second draft is now complete, but you still have two weeks of detailed, rather tedious work to do. Don't skip it—tedious or not, it is essential. Most of the books on writing assignments and reports devote a chapter to this, generally in the form of a check-list.* As you read this section you will see that, if you have used your word-processing program to its fullest, many of the jobs will already have been done. Also, if you have followed the structural framework I suggested in Chapter 2 and enlarged on in Chapters 6 to 11, you will find that you are just ticking the boxes in a large part of it.

Preliminary pages

The first few pages, before the start of Chapter 1, are preliminary pages that set the context of the thesis or report, and help readers to find their way into it. They will include some or all of the following, generally in this order:†

---

* See, for example, J. Anderson and M. Poole, *Thesis and Assignment Writing*, 2nd edn, John Wiley & Sons, Brisbane, 1994, ch. 14.

† You will find more detail on this in any good style manual, such as the Australian Government Publishing Service (AGPS), *Style Manual for Authors, Editors and Printers*, 5th edn, AGPS, Canberra, 1994.

Title page
Contains title, author, and place. If a thesis, you will need to state the month and year, and the degree for which it is submitted. Check with your university to see what else needs to be said.

Dedication
Optional

Abstract
Usually a mandatory requirement for theses. For long reports it is usual to have instead an 'Executive Summary'. In both cases you should include summaries of the three main components of the project, as outlined in Chapter 2:

- Why you did the work and what you were trying to achieve.
- What methods you used and what results you obtained.
- What you concluded from it.

Table of Contents
Sets out the main divisions of the work. It lists all chapter headings and headings of main sections within chapters. (Many authors also list sub-section headings. I suggest you don't—it clutters up the table of contents and robs it of the power to demonstrate the structure of your report or thesis.) At the same hierarchical level as the chapter headings should be any items between the Table of Contents and Chapter 1 (Preface or Acknowledgements), and all endmatter (Notes, if endnotes; References; Appendixes; Glossary).

All entries should have the page number on which they begin set beside them. It is customary to use small roman numerals for the preliminary pages; start a new list in arabic numerals for the first page of Chapter 1. As you may have changed things after completing the first draft, check that the page numbers in the table of contents are accurate. (If you use the *style sheet* method of generating your table of contents, it is very easy to generate a new one at any time, with the new page numbers automatically inserted.) You should set up new styles for all entries of your table of contents on your style sheet, as you don't want them to appear as they did in the text—all in bold, for example.

List of Figures

Check that titles of figures match those in the text, and that page numbers are correct. One way to do this is to copy them from the text and paste into the list. Even better, give the figure titles a *heading* style in your style sheet. You can then generate your list of figures by using the style-sheet method for generating a table of contents. Whichever method you use, you should change the style—a whole page of bold figure titles is dauntingly *black*.

List of Tables

As for the List of Figures.

Preface

Should give any information about the preparation of the report or thesis that you feel to be necessary, for example how you came to embark on the project. Prefaces are seldom necessary for theses. If you do have one, any acknowledgements should appear in it.

Acknowledgements

Contains your acknowledgement of help received in the execution of the research and in the preparation of the report or thesis.

Letter of transmittal

Reports should contain the letter of transmittal from the reporting body to the person who commissioned the report. It should be signed and dated. It often appears straight after the title page.

The main text

If you have been following the methods I advocate in Chapters 6 to 11, everything appearing in this check-list should already have been done. But do check. If you have just picked this book up, and have not been following my suggestions, I strongly urge you to use this check-list. If you find any of the suggestions puzzling, go back and read the chapter concerned.

Aim

- Can the aim be located from the table of contents?
- Is the reason for doing the work outlined?
- Does the aim follow clearly from this problem statement or rationale?
- Is the aim followed by a brief outline of the way you intend to go about achieving it? (This refers not just to experiments or surveys that you will design yourself, but to the whole of the project, including reviews of theory etc.)
- Do the conclusions you draw in the last chapter relate clearly to your aim?

Background

- Do the introductions to any background chapters clearly state what their function is?
- Is there any material in the background chapters that does not contribute directly to the later development of the report or thesis? (If there is such material, it should be relegated to appendixes, or perhaps omitted altogether.)
- Do the background chapters justify the formulation of the hypotheses or research questions?
- If you are using a case-study approach, does the reason for selecting it, and a description of it, appear amongst the background chapters? (It should not, as it is part of your experimental method, and such material should not be described until you have selected your method.)

Design of Own Work

- Do your hypotheses or research questions spring logically from your reviews of theory and/or practice or your preliminary surveys or experiments?
- Do you discuss the possible methods for enabling you to test your hypotheses or answer your questions?

- Do you explicitly select a particular method or methods, and justify your selection in terms of your review of possible methods?
- Do you explicitly design experiments or other research programs to implement the selected method or methods?
- Are tests for your hypotheses or ways of investigating your questions unequivocally built into your research programs?
- If you have decided on a case-study approach, have you justified this decision adequately?
- Have you justified the selection of your case study in terms of its representativeness or typicality or other appropriate criteria?
- Does the name of the case study appear in the title and/or aim of your thesis or report? (It should *not*. If it does, you still have not sorted out the difference between a study of something in its own right, and the use of a case study to investigate something else.)

Results
- Are the results of your experiments or surveys or other own work clearly presented and explained?
- Are the major trends or findings outlined? (You should not be discussing the implications of them while you are reporting them. For a short paper this might be appropriate, but for a longer report or thesis you should keep them separate.)

Discussion
- Do you discuss your own findings in terms of their implications for modifying or extending existing theory or practice?
- Does the discussion permit you to reach all of your conclusions?

Conclusions
- Are all your conclusions justified by the preceding discussion?
- Are you making new discussions while drawing your conclusions? (You should not be.)

- Do your conclusions respond to your aim, as set out in your first chapter?
- Are your conclusions merely summaries of findings, or do they draw out the implications of your own work in terms of improved theory or practice? (They should.)

Format

You will have to satisfy yourself that the format you have used will help readers to find their way through the report or thesis and, in particular, that it is consistent. Most books on writing theses or reports give a chapter or more to this, with strict rules about the numbers of spaces before headings, the underlining of major headings, the use of numbering systems, the spaces between paragraphs and so on. These books predate the word processor.

As I argued in Chapter 4, when you use a word processor, an entirely different (and vastly superior) strategy for formatting is open to you—the *style sheet*. When you use a style sheet, you label each paragraph (this includes headings) with one of a list of predetermined formats or styles. When you have a fully labelled document, go through it, either on the screen or on a hard copy, and check that you have not mislabelled any paragraph. Then ask yourself whether the format for each style is helping you to achieve your desired overall format. If you are unhappy with any particular style (e.g. the style for *heading 1*), just change this on the style sheet, and every paragraph in the whole document labelled with *heading 1* will be given the new style. You will not have to check for formatting mistakes: the program does all the work for you, and can't make careless mistakes. The only possible mistakes are in your labelling of paragraphs with styles.

Ideally, all of this should have been done long before you got to the first-draft stage. However, even if you have already typed a complete document without using a style sheet, it is still worth going back over it, and labelling every paragraph in it with a style. This is not as formidable a task as it sounds, because

the program by default will have already labelled every paragraph with *normal* style, and you will have to label only those
that are not to remain as normal text, such as headings or block
quotations. Once you have done this, you proceed to check, as
above, for labelling errors.

Figures and Tables

Check all figures and tables. All will have a *caption* that may
consist of several parts: a title (which will appear in the lists in
the preliminary pages); explanatory material that draws attention to or explains certain features of the figure or table; and a
citation giving the source of the material. I shall distinguish
here between figures (which includes graphs, line drawings,
plates, photographs and maps) and tables. In practice, all the
figures may be lumped together in one list and the tables in
another, although in the past it has been customary to distinguish at least two lists of figures: figures and plates.

All figures and tables

- Does it add an extra dimension to your ability to give a piece
  of information, demonstrate a trend or get over an idea?
- Is it simple or cluttered? Do the important points that you
  are trying to make emerge clearly?
- Does it, together with its caption, make sense by itself, or
  does the reader have to read the text to make sense of it?
  (One should not have to.)
- Do you draw attention to important points in the caption?
- Is there a reference in the text *before* the figure itself? (A
  possible exception is photographs that we might loosely call
  mood pictures. They have relevance in some non-specific way;
  might not be referred to in the text; and may appear any-
  where—although they still need a full caption. Use sparingly!)
- Is the title labelled with a standard *heading* style from the
  style sheet?
- Does the title appear in the lists in the preliminary pages? Is
  the title the same in both places?

- Have you acknowledged the source or the information on which it is based?

Graphs
- Does it have both axes clearly labelled?
- Do the axes have suppressed zeros? (There are very few cases where this is justified; see Chapter 5 for my argument.)

Tables
- Have you arranged it in some way that makes it more than a collection of data? Would the reader see patterns or trends? (There is no justification for putting tables in the text otherwise.)
- Have you considered relegating it to an appendix, and plotting the main trends as a graph?
- Do individual numbers have more than three significant figures? (If they do, you are in danger of giving more data but less information.)

Notes and References

If you have used the numbered notes system of references, and you have used your word processor to automatically number or renumber notes, you should not have to check that the note numbers correspond to the reference numbers in the text—the program does this for you. (Of course you should re-read the notes to make sure that you have not accidentally deleted the wrong one, and that you wish to keep the ones you have. You should also check whether any of them need to be revised in the light of revisions to the text.) The program will enable you to collect your notes at the foot of each page or at the end of each chapter or at the end of the main body of text (but collected separately for each chapter), before your 'References'. Give your list a heading 'Notes' (a section-style heading if at the end of each chapter, or a chapter-style heading if at the end of the text). If you have used the author–year system of referencing, you should have included page numbers in the text when you were citing a reference in a book, e.g. (Brown 1983, p. 217). Check them as you go through the text.

Whichever system you use, you should include a full list of sources such as papers in journals or chapters of books that have been cited. The list should be in alphabetical order of authors' surnames,* and should contain sufficient detail to enable the reader to find the material in a library. You should check your list for three things:

- *Is* it in alphabetical order?
- Do the entries conform to established style?
- Do all the references cited in the text appear in the list?

Quite apart from the inherent importance of this, you will annoy an examiner if you cite material and fail to list it. One way an examiner checks to see whether you know what you are talking about is to check the references as you cite them. Conversely, you shouldn't put references in your list of references *unless* you have cited them. So all of these have to be checked, one by one. Read your own text the way that the examiner would, checking the list every time you come to a citation. (When you are half-way through this, you will wish that you had been far more systematic when you were collecting the reference material in the first place. You'll do better next time!)

You should head this list simply as 'References' in the style of a chapter heading.† In theses and reports it is customary to place it after the chapters but before any appendixes, presumably on the grounds that the appendixes really are something tacked on to the end. As the appendixes themselves may have

---

* The only exception to this would be a list of references at the end of a relatively short paper in a learned journal using the numbered note system; here the list appears in numerical order of appearance in the paper.

† Some people prefer to call it *Bibliography*. A list of references contains only material that is specifically referred to in your report or thesis, whereas a bibliography may contain other material of interest, but not specifically referred to. For a thesis, *References* is preferable.

references, there is a case for reversing this order. If you leave the references in the customary place, you should devise some logical method for overcoming this problem, perhaps by having a short list of relevant references at the end of each appendix. Check to see that you have dealt with this problem adequately.

Appendixes

You may have ended up with a rather mixed bag of appendixes after completing your first draft. Some of them will have been written for very good and valid reasons to support material in the text. Others may be leftovers from earlier thinking, and because you were rather attached to them you were loath to throw them out. I have already discussed rules for the use of appendixes in Chapter 5. Check your appendixes against these rules, and throw out any that are no longer justifiable. Check the presentation of each that you decide to keep, as follows:

- Does it start on a new page? Does it have a title that indicates what it is all about? (Just calling it 'Appendix 3' is not good enough.) Is the style used for the title the same as that used for chapter headings?
- Is there a preamble that explains briefly what its function is and what it is all about?
- Does the preamble refer to part of the main text? If it doesn't, find the part of the text that it supports and make reference to it. If you can't find it, or if the connection is very weak, throw out the appendix altogether.

Glossary

If you have a glossary, it is customarily placed at the end, after all the appendixes. Some writers are tempted to put it up near the front, even in the text itself. Don't do this—it is a special kind of appendix.

13 Other Types of Report

Although the structure outlined in Chapter 2 is generally applicable to any document that reports the outcome of research or investigation, such documents do vary greatly in scope, purpose, readership and length, and this will influence decisions on what can be left out or treated very lightly, and what writing style might be appropriate. In this chapter I shall identify these differences, and suggest modifications to my recommended approach to theses to make it applicable to other types of document.

My suggestions are not just for inexperienced students writing their first major work. At one time I spent nearly ten years as an Australian member of the editorial board of *Fuel*, a major international journal. My task was to receive papers from Australian researchers and, with the help of referees, to ensure that they met the journal's standards for publication. I found that even the most experienced researchers seldom produced an acceptable article first off: often it was quite unclear what the writer was attempting and why, what the existing state of knowledge was, what the method of attack was (let alone why it had been chosen), or what in the end had been achieved.

The differences between theses, reports and papers

Theses

Theses (or dissertations or reports of student research projects) are produced by students as part of the process of qualifying for a university degree. Here the writer sets the aim. The readership is the examiners. Many students have a vision that they are writing their theses to inform the world of what they have done, but this is the task of a paper in a learned journal. A theses is in effect an examination paper written to persuade the examiners that the student should be passed. Usually the universities give quite specific instructions to the examiners as to what they should be looking for, and students should read these carefully before starting to write. They also should listen to what their supervisors have to say on their first drafts, as these same supervisors will no doubt have been examiners of other students' theses.

Students always ask me how long theses should be. My answer is that it doesn't matter, as long as you can persuade the examiners that you know what you are talking about. Most universities in fact set *upper* limits to the length of theses, typically from 20 000 words for a bachelors honours project to 100 000 words for a PhD thesis.

Reports

A report is usually commissioned by some person or body who wants to know something, or wants some situation to be investigated and documented. Usually the commissioning body or client will specify the brief: what should be investigated and reported on. The report should be addressed to the client, and it should respond to this brief. The underlying theory used as a framework for the investigation might be reviewed, but it is unlikely that new or improved theory would be developed.

Another type is the in-house report of a research organization on some topic that *it* has identified as being of interest.

The organization might circulate this report internally, or issue it publicly. Such reports might then be rewritten in a condensed form as one or more research papers in learned journals.

Reports may be quite brief, especially if they are of a fairly routine nature, but in some cases can extend to several hundred pages or even several volumes.

Papers

Papers are articles presented at conferences or for publication in learned journals. The authors set the aim of the work themselves, the only constraint being that it fall within the ambit of the conference or journal. Such papers obviously should be addressed to those who will attend the conference or who will read the journal—which may well be a rather large community of interested people.

Papers will nearly always emphasize the development of new ideas or new theories. They are limited in length by the policies of the conference organizers or the editorial committees of the journals, usually in the range of 3000 to 10 000 words. This means that you will have to omit much material that would have appeared in an account of the work in a report or thesis.

I have directed Chapters 4 to 12 principally towards writing theses, and shall not go over that ground again. In the next two sections I shall describe the differences in approach required for reports and papers.

Writing reports

First, let us look at the more straightforward type of report, the internal report of some research organization. You should organize these exactly as I have suggested in Chapter 2. The only decision will be the level of detail to be included. There is no word limit, the readership is limited, and one of the purposes, at least for the first draft, is to get criticism from inside the research organization. As a result, such reports will tend to err on the side of allowing excessive detail rather than cutting it to the bone. This is probably a mistake, as the real conclusions may be smothered in a mass of detail. It is better to attempt critical thinking at this stage, and to relegate detailed data to appendixes, where it will form a permanent record of the research without cluttering up the report.

A more tricky type of report is the one written to describe work done in response to a brief from a client. I recommended in Chapter 6 that the first item in the introductory chapter of any research report should be a statement of the research problem. A succinct, one-sentence statement of the aim of the report should follow, and then a brief summary of the research approach to be adopted to achieve this aim. However, when you are writing a report responding to a brief, you will have to modify this order of development—the driving force of the work is not a problem identified by you, the researcher, but rather a request made by a client.

For this reason you will have to announce the brief first. Nevertheless, it is essential that, when structuring the report, you make the real aim clear. The brief will often contain several different requirements: review this, examine this, evaluate this, and so on. These separate requirements can't all be the aim of the report (as with theses, reports are likely to lack clarity if they have more than one overall aim). It is therefore advisable, before you start to write (or to do the necessary research, for that matter), to decide which of the several requirements in the brief is the real aim, and which are merely steps in the method you intend to use to achieve that aim. Almost certainly the client will have been indulging in a bit of thinking about how the perceived problem is to be dealt with, and some of the items in the brief will, in fact, be steps in the method the client feels should be used to achieve this aim. This may be a bit messy, as the client may not have thought out the method too well, and the first thing to do when carrying out an investigation should always be to negotiate the exact terms of the brief with the client.

I shall assume here that you did this before the research started, and you now have a brief that is part aim and part method. The first item in the introduction must be a statement of the brief. You should follow this with a short explanation of how you see the brief being tackled so as to satisfy the client, while still ending up with the clearest possible development of the report. This explanation will be a statement of the method you intend to use in writing the report, but interwoven with it will be your perception of the research problem.

You should then structure the body of the report in such a way that you meet all the requirements of the brief. For example, a requirement of the brief that turned out to be a step in the research method might have a chapter devoted specifically to it, and the conclusions to the chapter would be the response to that particular requirement of the brief. The penultimate chapter, the discussion, is then the one that enables you to achieve the overall aim.

In the last chapter, the conclusions, you should recollect the brief, and assure the reader that its requirements have been met. As the brief usually has several requirements in addition to the aim, it will be necessary to spend the first part of the conclusions reminding the reader where you have satisfied some of the requirements earlier in the report. Then will follow the conclusions you have drawn about the overall aim.

Writing papers

The paper often is the next step after writing an internal report or a thesis.* The same work is being reported, but to a wider

---

* I am confining myself to a brief examination of how papers should be structured. Many journals require papers to be presented in a house style, which they outline in a notice to potential contributors at the front or back of every copy of the journal. If you fail to follow the house style in your submission, at the very least it will delay publication; at the worst it will prevent it. An excellent account of all aspects of writing papers is given by David Lindsay in his book *A Guide to Scientific Writing*, Longman Cheshire, Melbourne, 1984.

and often more critical readership. Often the thesis or long report will give rise to two or more papers, each of which will focus on specific aspects of the larger work.

When you write a paper, you will not have to convince your readers that you know what you are talking about—that is not the function of a paper. Indeed, it will not get into print unless you have already convinced referees used by the publication committee. You are limited to a few thousand words, and you will have to leave out a lot of material that you included in the original report or thesis. Although you will follow the same general structure, you will be forced to take a lot of things for granted. You will include the introduction, but will have to cut it to the bone. You will include any necessary review of previous theory here, but will have to be satisfied with bald statements about your interpretations of it. You must reference it well enough for readers to be able to follow it up and make their own interpretations. You will end this introduction with a statement of the aim of the paper.

You will now most likely skip to your own work, because this, and the interpretations of it, are what will interest your readers most. How much should you include? The usual test is that there must be enough detail for a sceptical reader to be able to repeat your work. You will now go on to the discussion and conclusions (some journals require you to state your conclusions in an abstract or summary at the start of the paper, and in this case the discussion, which justifies these already-stated conclusions, will end the paper).

I must emphasize that the reader is not in the slightest interested in any demonstration that you know what you are talking about—this is taken for granted. But should you demonstrate that you *don't* know what you are talking about, you will most likely be attacked in a letter to the editor of the journal, or in a paper attempting to rebut your ideas. So even though you don't have to spend too many of your precious words demonstrating that you have done things properly, it is essential that in fact you have!

14 Joint Authorship

In your professional life you will write many reports or papers as sole author, but eventually circumstances will push you towards joint authorship. In recognition of this, our department has for many years required students doing the Master of Environmental Studies by coursework to cap their studies with a joint research project—with, of course, a joint research report.

The earlier chapters, addressed to individual authors, will also hold for joint authors—except, of course, that two or more people are making the decisions. It has been my experience that in the research business two heads are better than one, and that this carries through into the writing stage. But there are difficulties and, if your joint work is to be really fruitful, you will have to acknowledge these difficulties and deal with them. Researchers who use research students or research assistants to carry out much of their research and contribute to the writing of the report arising from it, and then fail to acknowledge their contribution by joint authorship, will not do it too often—the supply of assistants or students will mysteriously dry up. And a researcher who asks a colleague for advice or help and fails to acknowledge this contribution adequately should not bother to ask a second time!

I shall make some suggestions as to the protocols for reportage of joint work. But these are no more than the commonly accepted rules that permit people to work cordially together. It is far more important to recognize that each of the parties in a joint enterprise will bring to it strengths and weaknesses, and the outcome will be good only when each party contributes from his or her strengths rather than weaknesses. In short, a good professional relationship is far more important than a set of rules.

Group dynamics

Joint authorship should not even be considered unless each of the parties has something to bring to the enterprise. The *first problem*, then, is to ensure that what each has to offer is recognized by the others. Why should this be a problem? Unfortunately, personal power relationships often intrude. The most obvious case is the relationship of postgraduate students to supervisors. All through the project the supervisor has been in the role of teacher and critic. But, imperceptibly, students come to see not only the weaknesses in the positions of other people in the field but also, perhaps with a bit of puzzlement, the weaknesses in their own supervisor's position. This is not to say that meaningful supervision is no longer possible, but rather that it will change its character. But will the supervisor recognize this when it comes to writing up part of the work in the form of a paper? Another situation is that between two researchers in the same organization with similar standing as researchers, but in different positions in the hierarchy. In each of these situations, how will the authors decide who does what in the writing of the paper? How will they resolve disagreements over what should be written at a certain point? Perhaps most critically (because of its symbolism), whose names will appear on the paper, and in what order? The dominant partner is likely not even to see the problem—and will simply assume the decision-making role.

The *second problem* is more subtle, and probably more important. How will the authors meld the various contributions so that the sum is greater than its parts? Clearly they cannot tackle this second problem until they solve the first.

I shall point to solutions to these two problems later in this chapter where I deal with the various types of joint authorship. The common point is that there *is* a problem, almost inevitably, because organizational position and social dominance in the group are unlikely to match exactly the research insights and writing skills of the members. Unless the problem is acknowledged, especially by the dominant party, solution is not possible.*

Group reports

Commissioned reports

Large organizations usually have mechanisms for dealing with the problem of contributions from more than one author, but in smaller organizations these mechanisms may not exist. A good example would be an investigation commissioned from a university that drew skills from two departments.

Many commissioned reports require contributions from several disciplines, and therefore from several authors. An environmental impact statement prepared for the proponent of a major project is a good example of such a report—the disciplines involved include biology, botany, meteorology, chemistry, several branches of engineering, hydrology, geology, economics and environmental planning. A large firm of planning consultants writing such a report will appoint a project leader whose responsibility is to identify all the required contributions

---

* A cynical colleague of mine in the research and development department of a large organization used to insert one or two blatant spelling errors into all of his reports so that our boss would pick them up triumphantly, correct them, and leave the rest of the report alone. Group dynamics at work! The sum here was never going to be greater than its parts.

and where possible to appoint staff in-house to carry out tasks and write sections of the report, to hire sub-consultants to prepare sections of the report that the firm can not handle, and to schedule and supervise all the tasks in such a way as to produce the finished report by the required date. The project leader will also assemble the report and check it for consistency and continuity, perhaps with the help of an editor. All members of the team are answerable to the project leader, who in turn assumes responsibility for the successful preparation of the report. Lines of communication and responsibility are clear with this arrangement: everyone knows what their task is, and who will settle arguments.

This arrangement successfully deals with the first problem of group dynamics identified above. However, it certainly does not guarantee a solution to the second problem, that of melding the individual contributions. It may well do the opposite: the strong mechanism for allocating tasks and settling arguments may eliminate fruitful disagreement and leave the individual parts unintegrated. Our example illustrates this point well. The average environmental impact statement is a compendium of fine and useful information if one wishes to understand the impacts of the project on the local hydrology or bird life, but much interpretation outside the report is usually needed to determine whether the project should go ahead in the proposed form. I am not suggesting that a good project leader can not produce an integrated report, but the danger is there: the firm appoints such leaders for their skills in getting the job finished on time (in the language of Chapter 3, their skills of rational thinking and writing), and they are likely to be less good at seeing the problem as a whole (non-rational or creative thinking and writing). If I were advising a large firm on report writing, I might suggest they appoint *two* project leaders, one of each kind, each with his or her own brief, and let the 'fruitful disagreements' be focussed on these two.

The report with contributors from more than one discipline but no project leader may suffer from the opposite problem.

There may be plenty of fruitful disagreement, but it may be *so* fruitful that the project team cannot finish the report on time. It is no-one's responsibility to ensure that schedules are adhered to, and any attempt by one of the parties to hound the others may lead to ill-feeling and the collapse of the whole project.

This is one reason why universities have tended to set up consulting branches. The stated task of the consulting branch is to act as a first point of enquiry for consulting work, and to identify appropriate experts within the university to carry out the work (including multidisciplinary teams where appropriate, which individual departments might not think of). However, they will also act as project managers, albeit in a less inter-ventionist way than in a normal consulting firm, and act as a buffer between the various contributors. However, I suspect that they will not feel themselves to be in a strong position if the report preparation runs into trouble. The parties concerned should acknowledge the potential difficulties of group reports and put procedures in place before the work starts, rather than try to solve problems only when they have become serious. This should also apply to collaborative work carried out entirely within an organization such as a university department.

Student group reports

Project reports by groups of students present a particularly difficult problem. Universities set masters students the task of doing research and writing reports so that they will learn how to do it, not because someone in the university wants to know the answer to a particular problem. Unfortunately, many super-visors do not see themselves as teachers of research, much less of research reporting; rather they tend to leave the students to their own devices, and at the end make some judgement as to how well they have succeeded. With individual projects this approach can (and does) result in high dropout rates; with group projects the results are usually disastrous. Not only do the students not know how to do research or report on it, but they also do not have any idea of the problems of group work: they have both to master the problems of group dynamics, and to understand, accept and act upon each others' strengths and weaknesses. At the same time they are learning how to do research and write about it. Usually all of this has to be done in less than a year. The supervisor or supervisory team can expect problems almost as soon as the project starts, and should design a component of the supervisory effort to deal with this.

If you are a group of students in this situation, you should expect problems, and the first task you should set yourselves is to discuss the problem of working among yourselves, and to formulate a *modus operandi* or plan of working. You will change this many times, by mutual consent, as the project progresses, but the knowledge that you need one is the single most important lesson in group dynamics.

I have to say that I do not know of any sure solution to the problem of student group research and writing, and perhaps 10 per cent of students find themselves unable to cope. At best, the other members of the group in some way deal with the problem (and in so doing learn a lot). At worst, the group explodes, and the supervisors have to mount a rescue operation.

Joint papers

Papers written jointly by colleagues should present few problems. The parties have not come together through external pressures, but of their own volition. They would not have done so had they not believed that they brought complementary skills to the enterprise. Initial mutual understanding is, therefore, more-or-less in place, although often unspoken. Nevertheless, they should discuss this explicitly. Who is to write what? Who will keep the project moving? Whose name will go first? Who will deal with the editor of the journal?

I suggest the following guidelines. The person who suggests the collaboration should take all the initiatives and be the senior author. However, this person should also make the greatest contribution to the thinking and writing. If the initial discussions show that someone else will make the greatest contribution (this doesn't necessarily mean write the most words), then the parties should agree that this other person will make the running and be senior author. If it becomes obvious as the project goes on that the initial agreement about the project is changing, then this should be renegotiated. Don't let it drift!

When the paper is describing work involving a research assistant, it may be appropriate to have the assistant as co-author. This will depend on whether the assistant made a real contribution to the research or merely carried out work under the direction of the principal investigator. When the research assistant does some of the writing, he or she should always be a co-author. In all cases, follow the usual rule: discuss the *modus operandi* before the work starts. The principal investigator should always take complete responsibility for the paper, and should always be the senior author.

If you are a postgraduate student working on a research project, it is not necessary to wait until your thesis is passed before you attempt to publish a paper. If you believe you are on to something new, consult your supervisor and, if he or she agrees with you, try to get into print. But it is a tough game, and for this reason the convention is that you publish such material, either before or after the thesis has been passed, with your supervisor as co-author. This not only acknowledges the contribution made by your supervisor to the development of your research (and to your development as a research worker), but also commits him or her to a critical contribution to the paper.

At one time it was common for supervisors to style themselves as senior author in such publications, but this is now less common. Where it still occurs, in my view it indicates a mind-set which sees students not as developing independent research workers, but as research assistants. (Many years ago I saw a doorway in the chemistry building of my own university labelled quite simply '*et al.*'—the postgraduate students' room. As this label was done very tastefully in gold letters, the wry joke by the students must have been acknowledged by authority.) Of course there will be papers where the supervisor genuinely is the senior author; perhaps having made an advance in thinking as a result of work by more than one student. Even here the supervisor should be scrupulously careful to consult with the students involved, and to acknowledge their contributions appropriately.

Appendix: Some Notes on Grammar and Punctuation

Most readily available books on writing reports or theses deal with the art of writing—style and expression. They usually deal also with the conventions that support good expression, namely grammar and punctuation. This is not a book about style, but rather about structure and coherence, and I advise you to consult one of these books on good writing if you wish to improve your style.

However, I will point to two common problems, as poor writing *will* detract from the reader's grasp of the intended logic flow. There are two problems here. The first problem is *writing styles that hinder understanding,* even though they are not ungrammatical. In Chapter 5 I dealt with two of these: 'thesisese' and the overuse of the passive voice, especially when trying to avoid the use of the first person to describe what the author did or thought. The second problem is *incorrect grammar and punctuation.* You will recollect that some of my students accused me of being 'picky' when I insisted on the importance of grammar and punctuation. However, this is not a trivial matter. The rules of sentence construction and punctuation *are* rules—designed to assist us to quickly grasp what the writer is saying. Incorrect grammar and punctuation will not only require the reader to wrestle with what the writer is saying, but may well lead to an incorrect interpretation.

I cannot deal here with all the errors that I have come across in a long career of reading drafts theses and reports. I recommend that you *buy a good style manual,* such as the AGPS *Style Manual,** and *work with it at your elbow.* Such books will tell you all you need to know, in fact more than you can take in at first. Here I wish to do two things only: give you a sketch of the most common uses and misuses of punctuation, and give a brief account of the correct use (and common misuse) of conjunctions and transitions for linking clauses and sentences. These are not just niceties of style; they are basic tools for communication.

Punctuation

Comma (,)

The comma is the most used (and most misused) punctuation mark. I shall mention here only the five most common uses, and the two most common misuses. If you are not too sure whether a comma should be used, try reading the sentence out loud. Where you find yourself pausing momentarily, you should probably be using a comma. Where you don't pause, you should probably not be using the comma. Use commas for the following purposes:

- To mark the separation of an adverbial phrase or clause from the main clause:

    Before anyone types a single word, the curator of the master document draws up a style sheet.

    Also use between co-ordinate clauses linked by words such as *and, but, or, nor.*

    More recent programs check your spelling for you, and even make suggestions about your grammar.

- After transitional words such as *however, nevertheless, moreover, therefore, similarly.*

---

* Australian Government Publishing Service (AGPS), *Style Manual for Authors, Editors and Printers,* 5th edn, AGPS, 1994. In these notes on punctuation, I am generally following the recommendations of the AGPS *Style Manual,* and occasionally paraphrasing entries in it. The examples I give, however, are taken from elsewhere in this book.

- Between items in a list, except before the final *and, etc.* and *or:*

    . . . their own surveys, interviews, observations, experiments etc.

  Many people think that this exception means that a comma should never be used before the word *and.* This is not so: the rule applies only to the last item in a list.
- Between adjectives qualifying the same noun, except before the word *and:*

    Some people can write beautiful, clear, direct English that aids communication.

- To put a word or phrase in parenthesis. (To test whether something should be in parenthesis, try omitting the commas altogether; the sentence will lose some information, but should still make sense.) One comma must be placed before the word or phrase, and one after it:

    This included focussed interviews, lasting about one hour each, with three farmers.

  Brackets and dashes can also be used to indicate parentheses (see below).

Common *misuses* of commas:

- Use of only one when creating a parenthesis:

    This included focussed interviews lasting about one hour each, with three farmers.

  Two or none!
- To mentally 'catch breath' between a long subject and the verb:

    How one could be 'critical' in these circumstances, is quite beyond me.

  There should never be a comma between a subject and its verb. Sometimes the subject may be qualified by a phrase or clause in parenthesis, and commas will therefore appear:

    The detailed design of the experiments, and hence the physical design of the apparatus, required quite precise hypotheses.

  In such cases the 'two-or-none' rule applies.

135

Semicolon (;)

The semicolon is a *separator*, like a comma, but stronger. Its two main uses are:

- To separate parts of a sentence that are too closely related to be broken into separate sentences:

   Writers of thesisese nearly always use the passive voice; their verbs are activated by other verbs; their sentences are long and complicated; they prefer long and seldom-used words to the short equivalent words common in every-day communication; jargon is rife; and so on.

- To separate items in a list.

Colon (:)

The colon should not be confused with the semicolon. They have quite different uses, and cannot be used interchangeably. The three main uses of the colon all have a sense of *introducing* something that is to follow:

- To introduce a list, for example the lists of uses of the various items of punctuation in this section. The various items in the list are often separated by semicolons.
- To introduce something that will amplify or explain what preceded it:

   I did it: I thought through a whole sentence on to the screen.

- To introduce a quotation, although a comma may be used when the quotation consists of one simple sentence only.

Dash/hyphen (— -)

They are different, and each has its own specific uses. You should find out how to create both on your word processor.

- The *dash* (or em rule) has two principal uses: to indicate an abrupt change in the sentence structure, and to indicate material that is in parenthesis. It should be used for parentheses only when the break is very abrupt. Otherwise, use brackets or commas. As with all **parentheses, two** or none.

- The *hyphen* is used to build up complex words. The commonest are words built up from suffixes such as *sub-* or *non-* (incidentally, these suffixes should never stand alone as separate words). As time goes on, some of these complex words become words in their own right, and no longer need the hyphen (thus 'sub-zero', but 'nonconformist'). Consult your dictionary.

  Hyphens are also used to form compound nouns (e.g. 'grammar-check') and compound adjectives (e.g. 'light-sensitive'), often from a mixture of adjectives, verbs and nouns. Compound nouns are straightforward—but consult your dictionary to see whether words should be separate, linked by hyphens, or set as one word. Usage varies and is always changing. *Consistency* within any piece of writing is vital.

  Compound adjectives can be very tricky. A student once gave me 'sulphur reduced residual fuel oil fired brick kiln'. Where should he have put the hyphen(s)? Another gave me a 'non-cost of living indexed pension'. The first of these is a mixture of compound adjectives and compound nouns, some of which don't take hyphens (e.g. 'brick kiln').The best solution is to break it up a bit. I suggest 'brick kiln fired with sulphur-reduced residual fuel oil'. Similarly, I suggest 'pension not indexed for cost of living'.

Brackets ( ) [ ]

Curved brackets (or parentheses), and square brackets have quite separate uses. Don't use them interchangeably. And don't be tempted to use other types of bracket, such as curly brackets (except perhaps in mathematical expressions); no convention exists to indicate their meaning.

- *Curved brackets* or parentheses are used to enclose expressions that are not essential to the meaning of the sentence but that amplify or clarify or may be considered to be an aside. They are also used to enclose numbers or letters designating items in a list.

137

- *Square brackets* are reserved for interpolations. Their principal use is to make your own interpolations inside quotes from other writers. Such interpolations would consist of words you insert to clarify the meaning, or that magic word *sic* (Latin for 'thus') to indicate that the original author, not you, was responsible for an obvious misspelling or inaccuracy.

Quotation marks (' ' " ")

The principal use of quotation marks is to enclose the *exact* words of a writer or speaker, whether or not these form a complete sentence or sentences. Use *single* quotation marks. Use double quotation marks *only* for quotations within quotations.

There are other ways of indicating quotations, and other uses of quotation marks. These are the principal ones:

- Long quotes from the work of others, say longer than thirty words, should not be designated by quotation marks and contained within the normal text, but should be presented as a separate block. The whole block should be in slightly smaller type, indented, with space above and below. Quotation marks are not needed, and should not be used.
- Quotation marks (again, single marks) are used to indicate that the enclosed words are the title of a chapter in a book, a paper in a journal, a poem etc.
- Quotation marks are also used to indicate colloquial words in formal writing, or technical words in non-technical writing. After the first use of the word, the quotation marks may be omitted. Many writers extend this use by putting pet words or humorous expressions in quotes. It is best to avoid this as much as possible: it can become a bad habit.

Link words

We use link words to indicate the logic flow in a passage of text. They are of two kinds: *conjunctions,* which are used inside sentences to link clauses, and *transitional words,* which are used to link a sentence to the one that preceded it. Many writers seem to use them interchangeably. This is a great source of confusion. Let me emphasize that insisting on the correct use of words is not mere pedantry—it will help the reader follow your meaning.

Conjunctions

Conjunctions are used to link an adverbial clause in a sentence to the main clause. The adverbial clause defines the time, place, manner, or cause of the main action. They are also used to link co-ordinate clauses in a sentence; such clauses are related to each other, but one does not define the other in any way. Commonly used conjunctions are: *but, although, unless, if, as, since, while, when, before, after, where, because, for, whereas, and, or, nor.* If you are in doubt as to whether a word is a conjunction, and can therefore be used to link two clauses in the same sentence, check your dictionary. Conjunctions will have the abbreviation *conj.* after them.

In each of the following sentences the conjunction is placed in italics:

In such reports the underlying theory used as a framework for the investigation might be reviewed, *but* it is unlikely that new or improved theory would be developed.

In the discussion chapter the creative part of our brain is paramount, *because* this is the part of the thesis where we are still doing research.

If you are to become a participant, you will need to have some practical experience of your own.

When you have finished writing for the day, save what you have written.

Since this happened I have asked students to include all the preliminary pages when they submit their second drafts.

You will have two themes bumping along in your report together, *and* the reader will not be able to work out what you are doing.

Transitional words

Whereas conjunctions are used to link clauses within a sentence, transitional words are used to link one sentence to the next.

Commonly used transitional words are: *however, thus, therefore, instead, also, so, moreover, indeed, furthermore, now, nevertheless, likewise, similarly, accordingly, consequently, finally*. Some transitional phrases are also available: *in fact, in spite of, as a result of, for example, for instance*. A conjunction cannot be used to begin a single main clause; a transitional word always can. A conjunction cannot be separated from its clause by a comma; a transitional word can. Transitional words appear in the dictionary as adverbs; if you cannot find the abbreviation *adv.* after a word, then don't use it as a transitional word. (The words *but* and *or* are shown in the dictionary as both conjunctions and adverbs, and can be used as transitional words. The word *and* is only a conjunction, but is occasionally allowed to break the rule, and appear as a transitional word. There are no other exceptions.)

In the following sentences the transitional words are shown in italics. You will notice that each of the sentences consists of a single clause:

> *Thus* we see that research is a peculiar mixture of creative thinking and rational thinking.

> You have to be a bit careful of the word 'method', *however*.

> *But* this was not her problem.

> *So*, let me ask another question.

> *Finally*, you will report on the specific design of the investigation.

> *And* why might the attempt be beneficial?

The first six of the transitional words on my list are commonly *misused* as conjunctions, as shown in the following:

> In such reports the underlying theory used as a framework for the investigation might be reviewed *however* it is unlikely that new or improved theory would be developed.

> You will have two themes bumping along in your report together, *therefore* the reader will not be able to work out what you are doing.

The opposite fault is also not uncommon—conjunctions used as transitional words:

Although this was not her problem.

Whereas this is the part of the thesis where we are still doing research.

References

Anderson, J. & Poole, M., *Thesis and Assignment Writing*, 2nd edn, John Wiley & Sons, Brisbane, 1994.

Australian Government Publishing Service (AGPS), *Style Manual for Authors, Editors and Printers*, 5th edn, AGPS, Canberra, 1994.

Belsey, C., *Critical Practice*, Methuen, London, 1980.

Committee on Advances in Assessing Human Exposure to Airborne Pollutants, *Human Exposure Assessment for Airborne Pollutants: Advances and Opportunities*, National Academy Press, Washington, 1990.

Hoon, V., Himalayan Transhumance and Nomadism, PhD thesis, University of Madras, 1989.

Koestler, A., *The Sleepwalkers*, Penguin, Harmondsworth, 1959.

Lindsay, D., *A Guide to Scientific Writing*, Longman Cheshire, Melbourne, 1984.

McDonald, A., Long and Short Term Effects of Laser Grading upon Irrigated Agricultural Land in Victoria, MLArch research report, University of Melbourne, 1989.

Mutimer, G., Environmental Attitudes and Behaviour, BPD (Hons) research report, University of Melbourne, 1991.

Nuberg, I. K., Appropriate Interventions for Rehabilitating Degraded Tropical Uplands, PhD thesis, University of Melbourne, 1993.

Reynolds, L. & Simmonds, D., *Presentation of Data in Science*, Martinus Nijhoff Publishers, The Hague, 1983.

Thomas, G. R., Ignition of Brown Coal Particles, MEngSc thesis, University of Melbourne, 1970.

Wakeham, E., The Mining Heritage Landscape: Our Cultural Past, Present and Future, BPD (Hons) research report, University of Melbourne, 1992.

Index